ENCYCLOPEDIA

OF

Etiquette

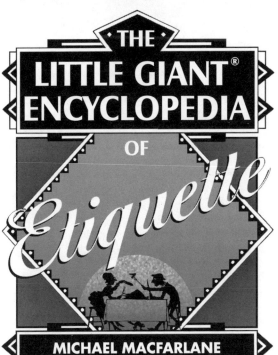

THE LITTLE GIANT® ENCYCLOPEDIA

OF

Etiquette

MICHAEL MACFARLANE

Sterling Publishing Co., Inc.
New York

Book design by Laura Best
Illustrations by Shauna Mooney Kawasaki

The author has strived to be as accurate as possible with the exact wording of direct quotes and with attribution to original sources. Our apologies in advance for any misrepresentation or inaccuracy due to the reprinting of sources.

Library of Congress Cataloging-in-Publication Data Available

10 9 8 7 6 5 4 3 2 1

Published by Sterling Publishing Company, Inc.
387 Park Avenue South, New York, N.Y. 10016
©2001 by Michael Macfarlane
Distributed in Canada by Sterling Publishing
c/o Canadian Manda Group, One Atlantic Avenue, Suite 105
Toronto, Ontario, Canada M6K 3E7
Distributed in Great Britain and Europe by Cassell PLC
Wellington House, 125 Strand, London WC2R 0BB, England
Distributed in Australia by Capricorn Link (Australia) Pty. Ltd.
P.O. Box 704, Windsor, NSW 2756 Australia

Sterling ISBN 0-8069-6847-8

Table of Contents

Introduction

The basic origins of manners and etiquette as we know them are purported to have begun in France. The word Etiquette is of French origin (circa 1750) and literally means ones ticket or conduct or procedure of persons of good breeding to be observed in social or official life. It is interesting to observe that proper dress and social conduct were deemed of great import in the France of the 16th century, long before bathing on a regular basis became personally endearing.

Here, we will consider the usual: where to place the dessert spoon, the rules of tipping, party invitations, and dealing with late guests. In the world of today, it also seems reasonable to address the etiquette of the Internet and a few tips on traveling abroad and the customs of other countries.

Beginnings

I did not begin with "in the beginning," although manners and etiquette may well go back that far. It is difficult to say exactly where the customs called manners actually began. The French lay claim to many; however, the traditions and manners of the Orient were refined when Europe was still lacking in personal niceties.

England of the 1800s began to formalize acceptable behavior, and much of it came across the channel. Protocols and the age of chivalry came before the gentler art of table manners and lace cuffs. Medieval Europe began to see a change in social behavior from fingers to forks and from slabs of meat clutched in a fist to morsels on a silver fork.

Manners evolved slowly as part of the class systems of countries—seldom being passed down to the working class. Behavior in the lower classes remained brutish and oriented only to survival.

Diplomacy

Convention & Protocol

Protocols allegedly began with relationships between tribes and then kingdoms and countries. Meetings, tournaments, and negotiations over land rights and borders needed to be formalized and rules defined. Knighthood and chivalry came at about the same time, with the noble ideals of the knight doing battle for his sovereign, his lady, or his cause. All were within well-defined rules, including how they could kill someone.

Of importance were issues such as an ambassador's place in a procession, and who entered the room first in negotiations. Some of these seemingly silly formalities still carry over. For example, negotiations between the United States (U.S.) and Russia in recent years have been delayed for days over the shape of the conference table and the doors through which each delegate would enter.

Negotiations to end the Korean War often were

delayed over such diplomatic niceties as who entered the room first and where they were seated.

People have argued and even waged war for centuries over status, class distinctions, and social standing. In many countries, perceived insult to royalty was a capital offense that demanded the life of the offender.

The etiquette and manners of diplomatic meetings, negotiations, and social events has been tediously prescribed. Position and seniority was carefully protected and revered. When countries or kingdoms first began to meet and negotiate for whatever reason, we began to see an exchange or at least a recognition of different customs and protocols.

Some of the first diplomatic relations were between tribes or families or clans living in close proximity. These meetings or gatherings, even though they seemed somewhat rustic and loosely defined, actually utilized rigid protocols as to who presented what to whom, where certain persons could or could not sit, and how leaders were addressed. The higher up the government or political ladder a person was, dictated how he or she was treated and what accommodations were made.

Personal representatives of a government would bear different titles, but sooner or later they became known as ambassadors.

An ambassador was a more personal representative of a government than an envoy or a minister. In addition to the diplomatic station, seniority was an important factor in international protocols.

Along with station and prestige, diplomatic position also brought privilege and immunities. We have all heard or read of the sometimes abused diplomatic immunity granted to visiting emissaries. This generally means the visiting diplomat, his or her family, and sometimes staff are not held accountable to local law and custom.

Until 1961, the property of a foreign embassy

was considered sovereign to the nation or country represented. While this is no longer strictly the case, the premises of a foreign mission or embassy is considered inviolable and members of the host state must request permission from the senior official to enter the enclave. This long-held principal was broken in Iran in 1979, when a group of Iranians invaded the U.S. Embassy in Tehran and held fifty staff members hostage for fourteen months. Some of the Middle Eastern countries, however, do not adhere completely to the idea of immunity; those who break their laws or codes can be very quickly and severely punished.

Language of Diplomacy

Early diplomats in Europe were church envoys, and as a result the language of diplomacy was Latin. With the increasing French influence on the European scene, the precision of the French language and the use of French in European courts, French became the language of diplomacy.

The U.S. entry into World War I saw the rise of English as a second language of diplomacy. The growth of the great and frustrating experiment known as The League of Nations saw official records kept in both French and English. After World War II, the organizers of the United Nations (UN) sought to have most sessions recorded in five languages: English, French, Spanish, Russian, and Chinese. At this time, however, most UN documents are published only in English and French.

Negotiations

We have come full circle in diplomatic negotiations. Early on, only the highest in rank could enter into negotiations on behalf of one's sovereign or country. Now, there are special envoy selected more often than not, depending upon the situation and the need, regardless of formal credentials.[1] While we are more concerned with the niceties of negotiations than the history, we will pause here and go into detail on other etiquette issues.

Addressing by Title

Titles are usually won or earned quite honestly, and the people wearing a title (with a few exceptions) take them seriously. If in a formal setting with titled persons, it is well to know how to address them. The more at ease you become with the rules of etiquette, the more relaxed you will act in these situations, and the more natural proper behavior will be. Following is a list of titles and instructions on how to greet each one.

- Air Force or Army U.S. officer—is addressed by rank, with the rank name first, e.g. Captain David Jones. Enlisted personnel are introduced as John H. Doe, Corporal U.S. Army.

- Ambassador, American—is addressed as Mr. or Ms. Ambassador and introduced as The Honorable.

- Ambassador, Foreign—is addressed as His or Her Excellency and introduced as the French or British Ambassador.

- Archbishop, Catholic—is addressed as Your Grace or Your Excellency and introduced as His Excellency or His Grace, or The Most Reverend.

- Archimandrite, Eastern Orthodox—is addressed as Reverend Sir and introduced as The Very Reverend.

- Associate Justice of the Supreme Court—is addressed as Mr. or Ms. Justice and introduced as The Honorable Justice Thomas White of the Supreme Court.

- Attorney General—is addressed as Mr. Graham or Ms. Williams and introduced as The Honorable Jan Graham, Attorney General or The Attorney General.

- Bishop, Methodist—is addressed as Bishop Allen and introduced as The Reverend William Allen, Methodist Bishop.

- Bishop, Protestant—is addressed as Bishop Smith and introduced as The Right Reverend Alvin Smith.

- Bishop, Roman Catholic—is addressed as Bishop or Your Excellency and introduced as The Most Reverend or The Right Reverend.

- Cabinet Member—is addressed as Mr. or Ms. Secretary and introduced as The Honorable John Smith, Secretary of the Army.

- Canon—is addressed as Canon or Reverend and introduced as The Reverend Adam Smith, Canon of . . .

- Cantor—is addressed as Cantor or Sir and introduced as Cantor Goldman.

- Cardinal—is addressed as Cardinal and introduced as His Eminence, Cardinal O'Rourke.

- Chief Justice of the Supreme Court—is addressed as Mr. or Madam Chief Justice and introduced as The Chief Justice of the United States, The Chief Justice, or The Right Honorable.

- Clergyman, Protestant—is addressed as Reverend, or The Reverend Doctor if they have earned a Doctorate and introduced as The Very Reverend.

- Dean, Protestant—is addressed as Dean and introduced as The Very Reverend.

- Governor—is addressed as Governor and introduced as The Honorable Governor Smith of the State of Wyoming.

- House of Representatives, member of—is addressed as Mr. or Ms. or Congressman or Congresswoman and introduced as The Honorable.

- Judge—is addressed as Judge or Your Honor and introduced as The Honorable . . . and then list the title of district, appellate, etc.

- King—is addressed as Your Majesty and introduced as His Majesty the King.

- Marine Corps, U.S. officer—is treated the same as officers and enlisted personnel of the Air Force and the Army.

- Mayor—is addressed as Mayor and introduced as The Honorable David Jones, Mayor of Inkblot, California.

- Member of Parliament—is addressed as Mr., Mrs., Ms., or Sir or Madam and introduced as The Honorable Chauncy Doright, M.P.

- Monsignor—is addressed as Monsignor and introduced as The Right Reverend Monsignor or The Very Reverend Monsignor.

- Navy U.S. enlisted personnel—are addressed by rank and name or as Mr., Miss, or Ms. and introduced by rank then name.

- Navy U.S. officer—is treated the same as officers of the Air Force and the Army.

- Patriarch, Eastern Orthodox—is addressed as Your Holiness and introduced as His Holiness The Ecumenical Patriarch of Constantinople.

- Pope—is addressed as Your Holiness or Most Holy Father and introduced as His Holiness The Pope, or His Holiness, Pope John.

- President of The United States—is addressed as Mr. President or Madam President and introduced as The President of the United States.

- Priest, Roman Catholic—is addressed as Father and introduced as The Reverend Father John O'Brien or Father John O'Brien.

- Queen—is addressed as Your Majesty and introduced as Her Majesty, The Queen.

- Rabbi—is addressed as Rabbi or, if holding a doctorate, Doctor and introduced as Rabbi Goldman.

- Secretary General of the United Nations—is addressed as Mr. Secretary or Madam Secretary and introduced as His or Her Excellency Jeff Marsh Secretary General of The United Nations.

- Senator—is addressed as Senator and introduced as The Honorable John Smith, the United States Senate.

- Speaker of the House of Representatives—is addressed as Mr. Speaker or Madam Speaker and introduced as The Honorable Adam Margetts, The Speaker of the House of Representatives.

- Vice President of The United States—is addressed as Mr. Vice President or Madam Vice President and introduced as The Vice President or The Honorable Albert Gore, The Vice President of the United States.

United States Flag & National Anthem

The etiquette of displaying and honoring the Flag of the United States is more than a concern for etiquette. The Flag is a symbol of all we are and stand for. There have been heated debates over the Flag and the treatment of the Flag, but I shall write here in support of honoring and properly displaying our national symbol and banner. A great many businesses and a growing number of homes now own and fly the Flag on holidays and other occasions. Many of these Flags are flown or displayed incorrectly. Here are a few simple rules for how and when to display the national Flag.

- Never fly the Flag upside down, except as a distress signal.

- Do not let the Flag touch the ground or water.

- Raise the Flag quickly but lower it from the flagpole slowly and reverently.

- Display the Flag outdoors only from sunrise to sundown. Lower and retrieve when raining. When flying the Flag at night, it must be lighted.

- City or state flags flown from the same staff or flagpole should be flown below the U.S. Flag. No other flag is ever flown above it.

- When other flags are flown on adjacent flagpoles, the national Flag is hoisted first and is the last to come down, except if it rains. All flags should be flown to the left of the U.S. Flag.

- When flags of other nations are flown, they are flown on separate standards. The flags should be the same size and flown at the same height.

- A Flag flown from a window sill or the front of a building should be flown with the Union (blue field with stars) at the peak of the staff, unless the Flag is at half-staff or half-mast. Flags are flown at half-mast only by federal, state, or city order.

- When the Flag is displayed without a flagpole, it should be flat against an upright support or wall. The Flag should never be draped or festooned. The Union section should always be uppermost to the Flag's own right.

- The Flag displayed over a street should hang vertically with the Union to the north in an east/west street or east in a north/south street.

- If displaying the Flag over a speaker's platform, it should be behind and above the speaker with the Union to the Flag's right, the observer's left. If the Flag is on a staff, it should be to the speaker's right. The Flag should never be draped over the speaker's podium or laid flat on a table.

- Flags carried in a mourning procession are never carried at half-mast, but may be adorned with a black knot or streamer. The streamers may only be attached by order of the President.

- When the Flag is to be flown at half-mast, it is first hoisted to the peak and then lowered. In the evening when the Flag is lowered, it is first hoisted again to the peak and then retrieved.

- On Memorial Day the Flag can be flown at half-mast from sunrise until noon, then it is raised to full staff.

- Do not use the Flag to unveil monuments or statues, even if they are patriotic in nature.

- One exception to the rule of draping the Flag is on a coffin. The Flag may then be draped with the Union at the head and over the left shoulder of the deceased. The Flag is not to touch the ground or be lowered into the grave. The Flag is to be used in this manner only at the funerals of members of the military and certain government officials. However, it is often used for former military members or veterans at the request of family. At a military funeral, the Flag ceremony is often accompanied by a rifle salute and the folding of the Flag. After the Flag is appropriately folded, it is presented to the spouse or family member of the deceased.

- When a Flag becomes worn, torn, or tattered to the point it is no longer appropriate to fly, it must be burned in its entirety. This ceremonial burning is interesting to observe, and should be done with seriousness and reverence, and is often performed by military units or Boy Scout troops.

- The U.S. Flag is never used in a ceremony to acknowledge any person or thing.

- No object or emblem should be placed above the Flag as displayed on a wall or on a staff except the American Eagle on the top of a staff.

- The Flag should not be draped on any vehicle.

- The Flag should not be used to cover a ceiling.

- The Flag should never be used as a decoration

for clothing, napkins, etc. It should be used only on official stationery never on personal stationery.

- No lettering should be placed on the Flag.

- Store the Flag in such a way that it will be free from moths or other damage; and never allow it to touch the floor. Do not allow anyone to step on the Flag or deface it in any way.

- In a public gathering or ceremony where an invocation or prayer is given, the prayer always precedes the salute of the Flag or the National Anthem. The rule still is God, then country.

- When the Flag passes by or is presented and the National Anthem is played or the Pledge of Allegiance recited, civilians should place their right hand over their heart; military or uniformed law enforcement officers should salute. A lady does not remove her gloves to salute the Flag since they are a part of her apparel, neither does a military person.

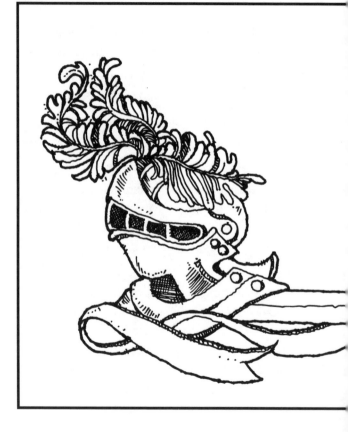

Chivalry

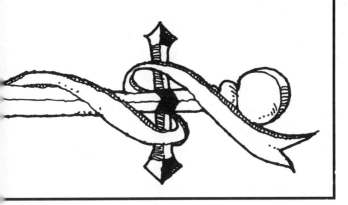

Chivalry—Its Origin

While chivalry did not begin as a measure of the manners of a gentleman, it has come to be associated with those manners in our understanding of knighthood and how man should conduct himself.

Chivalry was the code of behavior for the medieval knights—or rather it was the outgrowth or civilizing of what was originally a military necessity for the kings and feudal lords.

As a result of too many beatings on the battlefield and being on the wrong end of plunderings, the Europeans began training their warriors as cavalry. To maintain these warriors, the lord or king gave the warrior land to pay for the cost of training themselves and others, and to keep the specifically trained horses and the entourage that went with them. The warrior was also expected to give a certain number of days of military service and to fight bravely and honorably.

This bravery and loyalty were the precursors of what was to become the code of the knights. A group that began basically as mercenaries, with refined manners, became the legendary and glorious knights of Europe and of the crusades.

The most famous and glorified were the—perhaps real, perhaps mythical—knights of the round table of good King Arthur of Wessex in Southeast England. To the brave and loyal behavior of the knights was added religious piety, courtly love, and all of the necessary social graces.

As chivalry began to soften the hard edges of feudal and territorial warfare, the knights were expected to treat fellow and opposing knights with respect, and not to persecute those who were considered to be socially inferior. The knightly ideal taught that the knight fought for Christian ideals, glory, and honor—no longer for mere profit. Most knights, however, were not given to passing up a profitable foray into someone else's turf.

Courtly Love

Like much of the information about the age of knights and ladies, it is hard to discern legend from truth. Courtly love supposedly involved the knight devoting himself completely to a betrothed or married woman at court. In his lady's name, he would then wage war or joust in tournaments.

Out of these courtly love interests came the great tales of the handsome knights slaying both dragons and rude uncivil fellows for the honor of the lady. Manners and etiquette became a great part of both the legend and the reality.

In addition to being a great warrior, the knight was also expected to embrace the arts and learn to write poetry, sing love songs, and play musical instruments.

Knight Life & Training

The life of a knight was not an easy one. We should all be grateful to them for pioneering the principals and precepts of chivalry.

A knight usually began as a page in the household of another knight. His duties were household duties like attending to the knight's clothing, his meals, and possibly his social calendar. While in his teens, the page would advance to the level of a squire. As a squire, he moved to the stable and attended to the knight's horse and his armor.

All this time, the page/squire learned the social graces and protocols of court, and also a great deal about warfare and weapons.

For that time, the education given to the page or squire was quite complete. The young men (several squires were apprenticed to a knight at one time) learned horsemanship, the art of hand-to-hand combat, the manners of court, the rules of dress, and most certainly how to conduct one's self before the young ladies.

The squires apprenticed to a knight also performed a more practical and measurable service to their master—that of a group of light infantry to surround and assist him in battle. It goes without saying that this was probably where the slow squires were separated from the swift and cunning squires. A squire could labor for a knight for many years without much recognition and continue to be a faithful squire/soldier/servant. However, the bright, the cunning, and the brave who performed some deed of great courage in battle could be dubbed, or knighted, thereby completing the labor and training for which he was selected.

The squire could be dubbed on the battlefield by being touched with the flat side of his knight's sword or be slapped in the face by his knight in another form of recognition.

Later this battlefield custom took a more civil turn by being performed at court. At that time, the new knight received his fief or land. As the ceremony developed, the knight would often also perform a Christian vigil and vow to uphold chivalrous principles.

Decline of Chivalry

The wonderful era of the knight came to an end slowly; however, the manners and traditions of all but the battle and jousting became a major part of the growing manners, customs, and etiquette of later centuries.

Warfare began to change in the 14th century with alliances between states and countries and the need for larger armies and epic battles. Alas, the day of the small army of knights and squires was gone.

In place of the knights waging war in small bands and singing love songs to the ladies of the court came large and largely unwashed bands of mercenary soldiers. The death of the knightly order was helped along by the great plagues of Europe, which killed thousands of people and changed the entire relationship of countries. In addition, the development of the English longbow made archery a more important part of warfare.

Finally, the development of gunpowder and the introduction of muskets and cannons to the battlefield did away with the mounted knight and his squires armed with sword and lance. After being blown off the battlefield, the knight became a ceremonial entity.

For a time, knights survived in this superficial arena, but the ceremony itself became prohibitively expensive as the armor and trappings and the whole atmosphere of the tournament became more ornate, more ceremonial, and quite useless.

Many squires who had the opportunity to become knights elected not to do so because knighthood had simply priced itself out of the market.

Legacy of Chivalry

The original intent of the knights in their shining armor had in reality suffered a mortal blow, but chivalry was and is not dead. Much remained of the chivalrous ideal. It, in effect, became affordable at court as taken up by all courtesans in the form of manners and customs but without the great horses, the steaming jousts, and the bloody battles.

Throughout the 15th and 16th centuries, the ideals of chivalry and the customs of the knights survived among the European nobility. The true importance now consisted of keeping the knights' tradition and the noble ideals of chivalry alive as a mark of social distinction for the nobility.

Writers and poets throughout Europe began to pick up the old knights' code as a model for all of the gentlemen of the court. Baldassare Castiglione utilized this knightly etiquette as the basis if his advice to both men and women at court. This work was first published in 1528. During the two centuries that followed, many more writers and advisors to the noble and the rich fashioned similar advice for both courtiers and worldly gentlemen.

By the beginning of the 19th century, the figure of the knight had become even more romanticized. Observers and experts on etiquette and behavior saw the knight as pioneering the concept of romantic love and expressing the highest ideals of Christianity and civility.

In the 19th century, romantic authors like Sir Walter Scott began to attribute modern manners to medieval knights.[2]

Modern
Courtesies

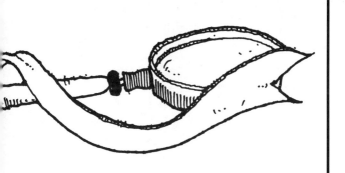

Origins of Modern Courtesies

Some specific manners and mannerisms began in the age of knighthood, such as tipping the hat, which began as a knight lifting his helmet visor to greet a friend, or removing his helmet altogether as a sign of safety and trust. The handshake supposedly began with the earliest of warriors extending the right hand or weapon hand in a gesture of friendship.

The titles of respect used today had interesting beginnings, e.g. the term Mister, or Mr., began as magister, meaning a ruler or lawmaker. As late as the 18th century in the United States, women addressed their husbands as Mr., rather than use a first name, especially in public.

Today, Mr. is simply a common courtesy term extended to all men. The women's courtesy title, madam, comes from an old French term meaning "my lady," which was used respectfully by the lower classes to address noblewomen at court.

The rules of etiquette have evolved from countries all over the world and have changed a great deal in some respects, while in other aspects remaining much the same for centuries.

Many of the first rules or manners had to do with inviting guests, serving them, and making them welcome in a home, whether upperclass or humble. One of the most consistent situations of etiquette has always been the question of sharing food and shelter with friends or strangers, and how it was best presented and received.

Among the Bedouin Arabs it is still considered ill-mannered to ride up to a man's tent without stopping to eat with him. Compare this to other attitudes about people who come unannounced and wish to eat. There is still among these nomadic people a long-established ceremony of brewing hot, strong coffee for any who visit. The Japanese still favor the old ritual of brewing tea for guests.

Rituals, both simple and elaborate, have always been used to make guests and visitors feel welcome. The early Greeks gave salt to a guest as a symbol of hospitality. Arabs poured melted butter over the hands of a guest to make them feel refreshed.

Today, in Arab countries as well as some others, one must be careful in admiring another's possessions, lest the host or host feel compelled to give them to him. As many have observed in film and other ritual performances, it was the custom among the Native Americans to pass the calumet or peace pipe. This became a symbol of making peace or forging alliances.

As people became more hospitable, as gathering places such as inns, public houses, castles, and country homes became more abundant, and as travelers and visiting dignitaries were received, it became more important how they were wined and dined. Hence, we begat table manners, which I will cover in greater detail later.

Table manners evolved quite naturally along with hospitality. The ancient Greeks did not use knives, forks, or spoons for eating. They, along with a number of other cultures, used their fingers for solid food, which had been cut into small pieces. Liquids were sipped or drunk directly from bowls or vessels or sopped up with bread.

The modern story is told of the boy who rebutted to his mother when chastised for picking at his food with his fingers, "Fingers were made before forks." His mother is to have replied, "Yes, but yours weren't."

The Romans—thought to have been very civilized—also took food directly from the platters with their hands. Some of the early Britons were to be seen ripping great chunks of meat from huge roasts or from a whole fowl with their hands and consuming it with great quantities of wine or ale.

Knives and forks were uncommon in Europe as late as the 17th century. People carried their own knives, which they used when great portions of food were served. Today, the use of the knife and fork still varies in different countries.

In the United States, the knife is held in the right hand and the fork in the left (if you are right-handed); once the food is cut, the fork is transferred to the right hand. In most European countries the fork remains in the left hand.

To a great degree, manners have always been considered to be for the upper class. Recently, education has become a reality for the majority of America and many other countries. Therefore, it is expected that most people understand and acknowledge some rules of behavior.

Many of the rules or manners of men have to do with their masculinity—their perception and acceptance by women or other men and in more modern times their perceived sensitivity and grace in a changing world. The perceptions of men over the centuries have changed; however, you must keep going back to the knights of Europe or the samurai of early Japan to understand the multifaceted expectation of what has come to be known as a "renaissance" man or woman.

The medieval warriors of Japan, or the legendary samurai, were governed by a code of behavior much as the knights were. They were expected to be strong, domineering, and invincible in battle, and then be warm and affectionate at the proper time and place. The proper place, however, was never in public, as he was even forbidden to show affection toward his family outside the home. In the unwritten code of the samurai, known as the "Bushido," one exemplified dignity, honesty, courage, and absolute loyalty to one's lord.

The ideal man of ancient Greece was the "kagathos" (the good and the beautiful). He was to be wise, just, and courageous as well as generous, truthful, and amiable. In this culture, modesty was of no import, nor was consideration of others.

Perhaps this is the reason for the first Olympic games being held in the nude. The perfect Greek also had to be especially handsome, since that people thought ugly was not ideal.

The overachieving culture known as Roman (or those proclaiming to be citizens of Rome) were expected to conduct themselves according to the "gravitas," a traditional rule of dignity. Vulgarity and boasting were considered ill-mannered to the Romans. Romans were to show respect to all men, even the poor and slaves, but especially to government officials and the aged. Personal appearance was less important to the Romans than to the Greeks.

After the beginnings of etiquette in 11th-century Europe, times changed as previously mentioned with the decline of knighthood as a form of warfare and the rise of the knightly custom of chivalry as the rule of behavior. With this change and acceptance of chivalry as the rule of behavior, the first books of etiquette were published. One of the most influential, *Il Cortegiano,* was printed in Italy in 1528. This was translated into English and the first English book of etiquette, *The Book of the Governour,* was published in 1531.

The dates of these "firsts" get a little muddy as the first English printer, William Caxton, claimed the *Book of Courtesy* in 1479.

Another first, *The Babees Book*, was said to have been offered in 1475. This volume was of great interest as it was published for young boys. The youngsters directed to read these books were instructed not to fidget when spoken to, not to spill food, and not to fall asleep over their meals. Manners and conduct began to be a concern in the Europe of the 12th through 17th centuries.

The Italian clergyman, Giovanni Della Casa, concerned with the rude habits and vulgar speech of the period, wrote *Galateo.* In approximately the same period, the scholar Erasmus wrote *De Civilitate,* a book of polite manners for young people.

In 17th-century France, social life centered on the court of Louis XIV at Versailles. The king himself wrote a book of rules for court ceremonies, which all his attendants were expected to obey. Even at this time and with the great divisions between the classes, the ordinary citizenry picked up on manners and attempted to imitate them.

However, across the channel in England, courtly manners began to fall out of favor. Now, mannerly Englishmen, in addition to being polite, were expected to be modest, pious, and compassionate, and to spend more time at their country homes than at court. The new idea during this period was that a gentleman should never be idle and should work for a living. We now see the growth of two schools of thought on the issue of manners.

One school still preferred the formal, courtly, and quite elaborate behavior and appearance of the French nobility, while the other embraced the more casual, yet quietly and politely elegant posture of the country gentleman or lady.

Remember that the ideal of etiquette began with the traditions of generosity and hospitality. The exactness of mannerisms of the so-called upper class came later. One wonderful example of a clash of cultures that ended up in mutual education was the settling of the Puritan colonies in early America.

The Native Americans who met the hungry pilgrims had a distinct code by which they lived. This code directed them to share even their last bits of food with the peculiar invaders from the big boat.

The Puritans, on the other hand, had a more rigid if not more hospitable set of rules. Immediately upon escaping the heavy-handed laws of England, they enacted their own set of heavy-handed laws against drinking toasts, bowling, and dancing, much to the confusion of the simple but generous natives.

The Pilgrims frowned upon most forms of

recreation and pleasure because these diverted attention away from religious matters. The first American book of etiquette, *The School of Good Manners,* appeared in 1715.

In the 18th century, manners were taught on a regular basis to most everyone who attended school. As well as learning to read, write, and cipher, it was now considered important to know how to behave and to present one's self.

George Washington, at the age of fifteen gathered his school notes and wrote a series of maxims, which became the book *Rules of Civility and Decent Behavior in Company and Conversation.* The young Master Washington offered such gems as "Give not advice without being asked and when desired, do it briefly." He also offered other tips about speaking above one's knowledge and public decorum.

When the English moved from the very formal French etiquette to the attitude of a patient and philanthropic country gentleman, there was one notable holdout. Phillip Dormer Stanhope, the Fourth Earl of Chesterfield, wrote a series of letters to his son advocating the more formal approach to personal presentation and his reasons for this direction. He felt that fine and formal manners were necessary to gain favor with influential people. Many thought this attitude far too selfish, but the work became very popular.

Another of Lord Chesterfield's weak points was his willingness to separate good manners from good morals. However controversial he was, Chesterfield also became popular in 18th-century America.

After the Revolutionary War, many in the colonies wished to make a break with English manners as well as English rule. Some new attitudes were established, but English etiquette manuals remained popular until the 19th century.

Among those who espoused Victorian manners in the United States and England, modesty was as much a part of the code as was one's actions at the table or at the ball. Men and ladies were questioned on their taste if they sat together on the grass, and it was forbidden for men and women to view nude sculpture in a museum together. Once again, economics, politics, and the changing world had a great bearing upon the accepted public manners.

After the American Civil War, a large and prosperous middle class began to emerge in the United States. Many lived in rural or unsettled areas and were thought to need some assistance in polishing up their crude ways. Along with the rush to wealth in this emerging land of enormous size, natural resources, and potential, also came a market for etiquette magazines and etiquette experts. It was at this time that magazines such as *Godey's Lady's Book* covered topics such as entertaining, kitchen management, and finally regular bathing for the general public.

Nineteenth-century and Victorian ways remained popular up to and through the period of World

War I. It is interesting how great conflicts and social upheaval tend to change and loosen attitudes about personal behavioral patterns. We would also see alterations or even abandonment of many social morals after World War II and the Vietnam conflict. In the postwar era through the 1930s, manners and morals underwent a great change.

With the advent of the motion picture, people saw the world of glamour, wealth, and beauty and realized it was indeed available to everyone. Women began to smoke in public, go to the "speakeasy," and emulate the freedom of men.

We also saw at this time one of the milestones of etiquette-and-manners advice. In the 1930s, Emily Post wrote *Etiquette in Society, in Business, in Politics and at Home*. The title was later changed to *Etiquette, the Blue Book of Social Usage*. This revision directed more advice and information to persons of modest means and took the need for good manners into every home in the country.

Classes & Class Systems

What began as a code of behavior or honor among small and select groups in Europe of the 11th century was now a consideration for every school child. The spread of kingdoms, states, diplomacy, the Industrial Revolution, communications and a number of rather significant wars changed the need and use of "manners."

Classes exist in most societies and are referred to as distinct social groupings, which at any historical period constituted what is generally called society.

While there are many measurements of social classes, generally they are separated by inequities in power, authority, wealth, education, positions of employment, religion, and culture.

During 11th-century Europe, and in many other parts of the world at that time and in subsequent generations, there were only two classes—the aristocracy, or rich, and the serfs, or poor.

The industrial revolution, world exploration, the changes in transportation, and other singular events produced a new class. The working class separated itself into two classes which are now defined as "labor" and "management." The owners, proprietors, and entrepreneurs eventually became the upper middle class, and by getting themselves landed and wealthy from trade and commerce, soon became the new upper class. The aristocracy then melded in from the top along with the newly rich from commerce, industry, and the professions.

However, the aristocracy were still noticed and envied for their manners and social skills. The idea of being a gentleman or a lady still appealed to the working, or commercial, class. At this juncture of the new era of "ladies and gentlemen," the bookstores and newsstands became full of etiquette and manners books printed on cheap paper like the dime novels of the day. One of the most popular was called *Beadles Dime Book of Etiquette*. Some of the genteel wisdom of these little treasures included:

- Never pick teeth or scratch head in public.

- Never pick the nose.

- Never smoke or spit upon the walk, to the exceeding annoyance of those who are always disgusted with tobacco in any shape.

- Never stare at any man or woman in a marked manner.

- Never scan a lady's dress impertinently or make rude remarks about her.

- Never jostle a lady or gentlemen without an "excuse me."

- Never tread upon a lady's dress without begging pardon.

- Never lose your temper or attract attention by excited conversation.

- Never dress in an odd or singular manner, so as to create remarks.

- Never fail to raise your hat politely to a lady acquaintance, nor to a male friend who may be walking with a lady; it is a courtesy to the lady.

- A lady will never be rude nor dress so as to attract undue attention.

- A lady will not allow her skirts to drag upon the walk to the annoyance of others.

- It is proper that the lady first recognize the gentleman.

- A lady is modest, discreet, kind, and obliging.

- Never swear or talk uproariously.

- A gentleman will never fail to bow to a lady.

- In offering a lady your arm, as it is proper to do upon the street, always offer her your right arm.

Impolite Behavior by Victorian Standards

- Loud and boisterous laughter.
- Reading when others are talking.
- Reading aloud in public without being asked.
- Talking when others are reading.
- Spitting about the house, smoking, or chewing.
- Cutting your fingernails in company.
- Leaving a church before public worship is closed.
- Whispering or laughing in the house of God.
- Gazing rudely at strangers.
- Leaving a stranger without a seat.
- Lack of respect and reverence for seniors.
- Correcting parents or any other persons older than yourself.

- Receiving a gift without expressing gratitude.

- Making yourself the hero of your own story.

- Laughing at the mistakes of others.

- Joking of all others in company.

- Beginning to eat as soon as you are seated.

- Not listening to what one is saying in company—unless you desire to show open contempt for the speaker.

- Speaking while one is singing or playing an instrument—a direct insult to the performer.

Victorian Etiquette for the Ballroom

With the revival of ballroom dancing, many young people have learned the various dances but are unaware of the old Victorian rules of etiquette still practiced in ballrooms today. Ballroom dancing is full of tradition, manners, and politeness. The following manners from the Victorian era are seen today in ballroom dance establishments.

A lady or gentleman should finish their toilet before entering the room for dancing, as it is indecorous in either to be drawing on their gloves or brushing their hair.

Always recognize the lady or gentleman, or the director of ceremonies with becoming politeness; a salute or bow is sufficient.

A lady should have an easing, becoming, and graceful movement while engaged in a promenade. It is more pleasing to the gentlemen.

To be proper, a gentleman should only ask a lady

to dance whom he has been previously introduced. If a gentleman should ask a lady with whom he is not acquainted to dance or promenade, the lady should positively refuse.

During the Victorian era, it was improper for a lady to attend a public ball without an escort or to promenade the ballroom alone. With modern dance clubs, ladies may come unescorted but it is still more proper for men to invite the ladies onto the floor.

An introduction in a public ballroom must be understood by the gentleman to be for that evening only, after which the acquaintanceship ceases, unless the lady chooses to recognize it at any further time or place.

A lady should never engage herself for more than the following set, unless by the consent of the gentleman who accompanies her.

Good posture and a correct and firm hold are the two most important features of ballroom dancing.

Poor posture not only gives an appearance of bad style but also seriously affects the balance and guidance of the dancers. A couple should literally move as one, striving for a smooth and relaxed motion across the floor.

The man always leads, while the woman follows. The man establishes the character and tempo of the dance. He listens to the music and is certain of the timing before he begins to dance. Nothing is more frustrating to a woman than a partner who cannot keep time to the music.

It is important that the man is aware of the figures dancing around him so he can lead his partner in a relaxed and confident manner.

Avoid being showy. It is far better to do a few simple steps well and with style than to stumble through a complicated routine.

If the man is dancing with a new partner, it is polite to take her through a few simple steps before trying something more advanced.

For progressive dances, i.e. the fox-trot, polka, or tango, it is customary to follow the line of dance. It is impolite and insulting for a couple to mar the pleasure of others by galloping around or inside the dancing group. Never go against the movement of the line of dance, which is usually counterclockwise.

If a couple bumps or collides with another while dancing, it is proper to give a nod, but do not disrupt their rhythm with a worded apology.

In spot dances such as the jitterbug or cha-cha, it is customary to stake out a small area on the dance floor where you will remain throughout the number. A problem arises when different dances are done at the same time. For example, some couples will dance the swing to fox-trot music so there is a combination of progressive and spot dancers competing for the same floor space. Courtesy would dictate a keen eye and quick movement to maneuver around the other dancers.

Country-western Dance

Today's country-western dancing has evolved from the combination of western swing and Victorian ballroom dances. The western swing is a version of the jitterbug done with more twirls. The promenade is a slow version of the polka. The ballroom dancers' box step has been adapted into what the country-western dancers would call the fox-trot. Slow dancing is popular with the country-western love ballads, which is much like the two-step. I must also mention the square dance, which is a popular form of the minuet.

Just as in traditional ballroom dancing, the dance line moves around the floor in a counter-clockwise direction. If you are moving slowly, stay in an inner lane and let other dancers pass you on the outside. The closer you are to the center, the slower you will dance.

If you are doing a stationary dance such as a line

dance or swing dance instead of a progressive dance, you should always dance in the center area of the floor.

Line dancers should never line up all the way to the rail and block progressive dancers. This gives line dancing a bad reputation. Even if the DJ called a specific dance style, someone else may want to do a two-step. If there are only a few popular line dances done where the floor gets filled, it is probably better for the progressive dancers to let the line dancers have the floor.

Line dancers should also be aware of those around them and aware that progressive dancers may be coming around the edge of the floor. The faster the song, the smaller the steps.

A hardwood dance floor should be treated with care. Drinks and cigarettes should never be brought onto the dance floor. When liquid is spilled on a hardwood floor, it leaves a dangerous wet spot. Even when it dries, this spot is pretty much ruined for the dancers the rest of the night because it becomes tacky and they cannot slide across it.

It is not appropriate to stand inside the rail on the dance floor to socialize. This is the fast lane on a country-western dance floor.

Be courteous to your fellow dancers and avoid colliding into people. Nothing looks worse than great dancers bumping into other people. Since the man is leading, it is his responsibility to keep an eye out for traffic. If you do collide, smile and look apologetic. You will usually get a smile in return.

If you are a beginning dancer, remember that everyone out there has probably experienced the same first-time-around-the-floor feeling. This will pass. If someone makes a mistake, the best thing is to simply smile and keep going. Everyone came to have fun. Hopefully, the experts at your club will be kind enough to give beginners the right-of-way. It may be fun to watch the experts, but it is just as much or more fun to watch the beginners.

If you have come to the dance unescorted, dance with the first person who asks. Once you get out there a couple of times with different partners, the available dance partners know you are unattached and probably won't turn them down.

It is my opinion that if you want to look western, you should not take country-western dance lessons from a ballroom instructor unless they have a very clear idea of the differences. I have seen many fantastic ballroom dancers on a country-western dance floor. However, it looks odd to see a rhinestone cowboy doing hand- and toe-pointing disco moves. Ballroom and country-western have some similarities, but the style in each dance is uniquely different.

Golf Etiquette

Etiquette is an extremely important part of the game. The etiquette golfers show to one another out on the course is one of the things that distinguishes golf from most other sports.

Golf requires a lot of concentration. If you are trying to make a putt, or hit your tee shot into a narrow fairway, it is difficult if someone is laughing, rattling their clubs, or running around.

There are a few rules of etiquette that apply in all situations on the golf course and the practice area; and there are other rules of etiquette that are particular to certain circumstances, such as the green.

The first and foremost rule of golf and golf etiquette is safety. Do not take practice swings toward another person. Avoid swinging your clubs when someone is walking around. Do not walk around where someone is swinging golf clubs.

Quiet is required on the golf course. Even if the

people in your immediate group do not seem to be bothered, there are other groups all around you. Walk, do not run. Running is distracting, and usually causes damage to the course. Walk quickly, but lightly.

If golfers have to wait too long between shots, they become impatient and they lose their momentum. Take only one practice swing for each shot, then hit the ball. Plan your shot before it is your turn. As you approach the green, determine in which direction the next tee is located and leave your clubs (or cart) on that side of the green. Never pull your cart onto the green.

When playing from a motorized cart, if one player is on one side of the fairway and the other player on the opposite side, drop one player off at his or her ball with a choice of a couple clubs, then drive to the next player's ball and meet farther down the fairway, after both have hit their shots.

If you are watching a partner putt, do not stand

in the shadow of his line and avoid walking between his ball and the hole. When you retrieve your ball, avoid putting your feet in your competitors' line.

Keep up with the group ahead of you. As they leave the green, you should be ready to hit up to the green. Don't worry about how far ahead you are of the group behind you, focus on staying a reasonable distance from the group ahead.

Some golfers get impatient if a group is playing slowly ahead of them; that is understandable. However, it is never acceptable to try to speed up that group by hitting a ball at them. If you are tired of waiting, walk ahead to their group and ask if you can play through—in a courteous manner and at a convenient time in the round.

If you are playing slowly and you think the group behind might want to play through, invite them to do so. When you are on a green, wave them up, stand aside and let them hit to the green.

As they are walking to the green you can putt out. Then allow them to tee off before you continue.

You do not need a driver's license to drive a golf cart, but you do need some common sense and respect for the course and the players around you. Drive at a moderate speed and be aware of other golfers. Keep carts on paths at all times—this is a rule that courses use if the ground is wet and they don't want tires to damage the fairway.

Under all circumstances, keep carts—motorized or pull—away from the greens and off the teeing ground. Often the course will post signs giving directions as to where they want you to park your cart; follow the directions. Courses become damaged due to excessive wear or overwatering, requiring greens keepers to direct traffic in order to repair damaged turf.

Manners & Customs in Other Countries

General Rules of Other Countries

There is not the space nor the amassed information to go into detail on the customs and manners of a great number of countries around the world. If you are going to travel to a foreign country it would be well to refer to your local library, travel agent, or consulate of that country for detailed and up-to-date information.

General good manners are always accepted in any land or part of a country. There are, however, specific customs or taboos you will want to be aware of before you travel. Many customs have to do with the basic issues of etiquette anywhere, such as food and dining, dressing for dinner, greeting strangers or hostesses, removing shoes, speaking too loudly or too directly, ignoring local religious customs, gift giving, and the consumption of alcohol.

Women should be aware of customs that specifically address women's issues in different countries, especially in the far east or middle east. If you are easily offended by patriarchal and male dominant rules, best avoid that country. If you do choose to visit countries with these hard traditions, don't try to change them to your enlightened way of thinking or you may find yourself on the wrong side of the law. Smile, make as many notes as you wish, and pass politely through the land.

Before traveling to a foreign country study the customs with regards to dress, food, religious holidays and observances, and the places to avoid.

If you are going on business and have associates in the country, call them to get the information you need, first hand. Go to learn and enjoy what is offered and not to instruct and improve (unless you are specifically asked, and then be very careful).

If you are going to visit several countries learn something about each. You may need to change your attitude and behavior as you cross borders.

The sections to follow are only a few examples of

customs and manners in other countries. There are hundreds of little phrases, movements, or actions that can offend or be misinterpreted in other cultures. The point is to learn something of the culture you are about to visit before you arrive.

As you view or hear manners that may be foreign to you, observe them quietly until you have an appropriate moment to ask a host or acquaintance what the meaning or origin of the custom or action may be and what your expectation will be.

Never remind someone from another country that we do not do it that way in "the states." There is much to be learned from others in the far reaches of the world. These wonderful customs and manners are best learned quietly, politely, and slowly.

Here are a few more tips, country by country, that may assist you. Remember, before you travel you will need to know much more than is listed in this book.

Argentina

Punctuality is appreciated in visitors for either business or social occasions. But expect your host to be a little late—this is common throughout all of South America.

Be prepared to talk about soccer or possibly music. Do not discuss politics or the environment unless you are asked—even then tread lightly.

Spanish is the official language, a few words will break the ice, continued attempts to converse or perform business with poor Spanish-speaking skills will not endear you.

The people are warm and outgoing—yet reserved. Accept all the food that is served graciously and always speak softly.

Australia

The Australians are proud of their country and not impressed with Americans who know everything. Do not tell them they sound English and avoid reminding them of their English ancestry.

When in a social situation, Australians do not like to talk business. When they are ready they will let you know.

They have a great sense of humor and a love of life. Australians are difficult to impress; even if you do manage to impress them, they may not openly admit it. Your best approach is to remain friendly, relaxed, modest, and unpretentious. Moreover, try to control any behavior such as nervousness, officiousness, or self-importance.

Maintaining personal space is important in this culture. When speaking to an Australian, try to maintain an arm's length distance from the person.

Touching, patting, or hugging other men in

public is considered socially unacceptable. Yet, it is common for strangers to greet one another and strike up animated conversations. Men should refrain from winking at or being too physically demonstrative with women. Point with your entire hand; pointing at someone with only your index finger may cause offense.

If you are invited for afternoon tea, you will get a cup of tea, but the invitation usually involves dinner also.

Although customary in this culture for men to sit in the front with the taxi driver, this is not the case for women. A woman traveling alone should sit in the back left passenger seat of the car; the driver will be on the right.

It is common for men to open doors for women, as well as employees for bosses and youth for elders.

Austria

Austria is not part of Germany. Much of Austrian food and drink, and to some extent customs will be akin to the German, but they are and wish to be a separate country.

Business practice and etiquette is basically the same in Austria and America; the major difference is the relatively formal atmosphere in which business activities generally take place in Austria.

The Austrians are punctual, and will expect the same of guests or business visitors. They are quite formal in manners. For example, when making appointments with prospective buyers or clients, it is recommended to make initial contact well in advance, either in writing or by phone, and offer to meet on the premises of the buyer.

Austrians prefer structure. Watch yourself and do not begin to eat before everyone else is ready.

Belgium

Here are the very delightful Belgians with a proud history of their own in art, food, wine etc., and sandwiched in between the French and the Germans. They may speak French or Flemish and are gracious and more informal than the French at mealtime or the Germans in a business meeting. A meal is a very social business and one should relax and enjoy the experience. The Belgians do not appreciate waste or excess, so to show respect, eat all that is served you.

Brazil

The official language of Brazil is Portuguese, not Spanish. There are some similarities, but it is a mistake to lapse into your high school or college Spanish and try to force an understanding.

Brazilians take their Soccer very seriously and believe they have the greatest team in the world. The fact is they are often correct.

In business, Brazilians enjoy conversation, jokes, and getting to know each other. In many South American countries, the socializing is part of the negotiation of business and is very important. You must take it as seriously as they do.

Brazilian food is more evident in the U.S. than before and more is being learned all the time about this very significant ally to the south.

Canada

Canada is our large and robust neighbor to the north and a very good friend; however, do not mistake a Canadian for an American, they are proud of their heritage and a country of more diversity than would seem the case at first glance.

Canada is, by law, a bilingual country and nearly 25 percent of the population considers French their first language. Much has been made in recent years of separatism for Quebec. Be aware of the very strong feelings. Most government officials in Canada are themselves, bilingual.

The Provinces of Canada are quite different in geography and custom from the Maritime Provinces to the great farm lands of the west.

China

When greeting the Chinese, always use the proper title of the person and expect a slight bow as you are introduced. Address a person using only the family name, such as Mr. Chen or Ms. Hsu. For business purposes, it is traditionally acceptable to call a Chinese person by the surname, together with a title. Avoid using someone's given name unless you have known him or her for a long time. Do not try to become too friendly too soon, and do not insist that they call you by your given name. Formality is a sign of respect.

A handshake is common, but not the normal greeting. Maintain distance when speaking to someone and avoid open displays of affection. Never appear loud or overly aggressive. The Chinese are quiet, but determined and strong.

When you are the host in China and invite

someone to a meal, serve a real meal and not just snacks and drinks. When a guest for dinner, at least sample everything that is served. Then leave something on your plate or the host will think you are still hungry.

At a formal banquet, be prepared to present a short, friendly speech in response to your host's speech. Avoid talking politics at social or business meetings. When given a compliment, it is wise to appear modest and quietly deny the accolade. Modesty is highly valued in China.

It is appropriate to bring a thoughtful gift to a business or social event. Gifts indicate that you are interested in building a relationship. Gifts should be wrapped; however, avoid black or white paper, representing mourning. Do not give a clock, handkerchief, umbrella, or white flowers as a gift, as these signify tears and/or death.

Denmark

The Danes are generally good-natured and quite informal. When introduced, they will shake hands in social, business, or formal gatherings. Of course, Danish is the formal language; however, most Danes speak quite good English, and the language is widely used and understood. Denmark is like many European countries in the restaurant customs. A gratuity is usually included in the tab, but a small tip is appreciated.

The Danes are punctual so arrive on time. When visiting socially, especially at someone's home, it is the custom to present a small gift of flowers or chocolate. Wine is also a good gift at any house party, but be certain what you are purchasing. If you cannot afford at least a respectable wine do not bring one.

England

When in England on business, emotions are seldom vented and the social climate may seem rather cool until you get used to it. In social situations the British may begin equally reserved and understated. You will find that the Welsh, the Irish, and the Scots are a bit more informal.

The British formality is a real issue. Even among well-acquainted persons in the country, official titles are always used. If a formal title such as a royal lineage or a peerage or knighthood is the case, the formal title actually seems to become a part of the person's name.

Business associates are becoming less formal, so on first meeting it is well to listen to the local conversations and greetings to hear what seems to be acceptable. Maintaining eye contact is necessary, especially when trying to emphasize important points. Speak in a moderate tone; talking loudly and shouting is unacceptable. It is considered appropriate to point toward your head, rather than directly at another person, to summon attention. A wide distance is often maintained between the participants in a conversation. Backslapping and hugging are usually discouraged.

Be punctual, it is very important both in business and social gatherings. However, you may be ten minutes late, but never ten minutes early.

The British, as a rule do not do business after hours unless a special meeting has been called just for that purpose. When work is finished, they prefer to keep the work talk at work and the social discussion becomes the more acceptable.

Getting an invitation to dinner in a business relationship is not as common as in other countries as the business entertaining is generally done at the public house, restaurant, or the gentleman's club. If you do get invited, flowers for the lady of the house are in order as is a nice box of chocolates—but don't buy Swiss, Dutch, or German chocolate, the English, too, are very proud of their own.

If in the course of the evening, usually at the beginning, a toast is offered to Her Majesty's health, you may smoke after the toast but not before. Whatever your feelings about the Royal Family, keep them to yourself. The British may take great leave to criticize their own royals, but that is not your privilege.

Entertainment is now replacing gift giving, this may be in the form of lunch, dinner, drinks at the club, or an evening at the ballet or the theater.

When wearing a necktie, avoid stripes as they may be copies of British Regimental colors; and that is not allowed if that is not your regiment.

Finland

In Finland, the sauna is a national pastime. An invitation to join a business or social acquaintance in those warm environs should not be rejected.

At a meal, as a visitor, you will possibly be the guest of honor. As such, you will be expected to offer a toast following the meal. Know in advance what you wish to say and have on hand a beverage with which to offer the toast.

As in any country, avoid drinking too much. Finland enforces the seat belt and drunk-driving laws rigidly.

France

The French are proud of their culture and history. Be sensitive to topics of discussion, table manners, criticism of food, and politics. The French expect you to have some knowledge and a great admiration for their customs and culture. The French are mindful of their delightful food reputation and table manners are most important.

The dress is often fashionable and professional, and social events are considered quite formal.

When dining out, avoid ordering a soft drink with a meal and do not put ice in your wine. The wine is usually served at the temperature designated for the wine and the occasion.

Do not ask for catsup unless you are ordering French fries. The French are proud of a wide array of fine mustards and sauces. Gratuities in France are included in the bill.

As in most European countries, with an

invitation to a home comes the expectation of a gift. The French have very good chocolate and of course, fine wine. If you wish to bring flowers, avoid giving a bouquet with thirteen stems as it is bad luck. Avoid purchasing chrysanthemums.

When greeted or greeting, expect a light kiss or on the cheek, it as a nice French custom.

If you are invited to a home for dinner, especially on a Sunday, expect several courses and a formal setting. There will be drinks or an aperitif to begin with, then the appetizer. Do not decline to sample a food as that is considered very rude. Avoid automatically reaching for the salt and pepper; this suggests that whoever prepared the meal did not get it right. The French hold the fork in the left hand and the knife in the right. When the food is cut the fork is not then transferred to the right hand. Each bite is cut one at a time, then eaten. It is very bad manners to cut the entire meat selection or entrée into small pieces at one time.

When at the table keep both hands resting on the table at all times. Custom suggests this dates back to other ages when some guests were carrying concealed daggers, so it was a sign of trust to keep one's hands in sight at all times.

If second helpings are offered, you should accept. By doing so, you will be considered a good guest; and in France this is important. After the entrée there will be a selection of cheeses. Save room after the appetizer and entrée to continue with good manners and sample the cheese. After the cheese will be a selection of desserts which may include chocolate mousse, French pastries, and various decadent and delightful morsels.

At the end of a meal, the French often serve what is called a digestive. This may be an alcoholic beverage such as brandy or liquor, or just coffee. In France, however, it will probably not be considered just coffee. Their selections are quite impressive.

Germany

Germans may not be too eager to offer an invitation to their home unless you are a personal rather than a business acquaintance. The Germans do have informal events at home such as cookouts and birthday parties. If you are invited to a formal dinner at a home or restaurant or wherever, it will probably be very formal.

The Germans are very good at entertainment and will serve excellent food and wine. In this case, the appropriate dress is very important for both men and ladies. If you receive an invitation, it should state what the expected attire will be. If you are not certain, then call someone and ask. With respect to everyday manners, the average German is still rather formal in comparison to an American.

By way of address, Germans will not be as quick to address someone by their first name as perhaps an American would be. The formal introduction and the formal use of the language will be used until they are better acquainted with you.

It is still customary to shake hands when greeting someone in German and this may be accompanied with a slight bow. The younger generation of Germany is beginning to adopt what they call the French greeting, with a light kiss on the cheek; but it is by no means a universal idea yet.

There is no longer a socially binding dress code except at formal receptions or traditional affairs such as weddings or funerals. Black is still worn at funerals. Men wear a coat and tie for business and women wear a two-piece suit or a dress. This is beginning to change a little; however, do not expect any of Europe to be as casual as America—with the exception of the young people.

When in public, men traditionally walk to the left of a lady; and when entering a building or going into a restaurant, the man enters first.

Greece

Greece is a country of rare beauty, old and new culture, great food, and a lot of pride. Be cautious, be calm, and speak softly. This is another of those wonderful countries where the merchants will gladly take your money, but a polite and respectful attitude will get you much further.

If you are doing business in Greece, give everyone your business card. When you want to say hello, don't wave your arm, simply raise your index finger with the palm closed. The warm climate allows for less formal dress, especially in the evening and at dinner. For specifics and rules of dress and the local culture, consult your travel agent. Greece is also a country with a degree of unrest from time to time. Before you travel, inquire of the local consular office or the U.S. State Department.

Hong Kong

Since the rule of Hong Kong was transferred to China, consider this as part of China when making any plans. Trust and respect are the watchwords in this part of the world. Avoid the colors blue and white as these represent death and mourning.

Foreign visitors will be forgiven for not knowing dining etiquette, just as they will be good-naturedly offered a knife and fork if their chopstick prowess is not up to par. Just as Chinese food, however, seems to taste better when it is eaten with chopsticks, so the entire meal will be more enjoyable if one knows a little of the ancient traditions and beliefs.

Although Western customs have influenced dining habits in Hong Kong, the majority of old traditions still live on. The guest of honor is usually seated facing the door, directly opposite the host. The next most honored guest is seated to the left of the guest of honor. If the host has any doubts about the correct order of precedence for his guests, he will seat them on the basis of age.

The host sits near the door, to be nearest to the kitchen. If the meal is held in the host's home, he will serve his guests, on the tacit understanding that they are far too polite to help themselves.

The use of toothpicks at a table is another standard practice. The polite way to deal with lodged food is to cover one's mouth with one hand while the toothpick is being used with the other. Toothpicks are frequently used between courses as it is believed that the tastes of one course should not be allowed to mar the enjoyment of the next.

The socially acceptable method for eating rice is to bring one's bowl close to one's mouth and quickly scoop the rice into it with chopsticks.

Hungary

Travel to this middle European country has increased greatly over the past few years. The food can be wonderful in the right place. Adults will greet you with a firm and often animated handshake. If someone has a professional title, they prefer it be used; other than that, Mr., Mrs. and last names are appropriate until you are well acquainted. When you are visiting, you may bring flowers or candy as a gift. When dining, the hands are kept on the table at all times, but not the elbows. Your napkin as also left on the table during the entire meal, rather than in your lap.

India

India is a country of mystery, great tradition, and now one of the educational and high-tech capitals of the world. You may travel to India for business as well as pleasure.

You will find the food quite wonderful, the customs exact, and the requirements for good behavior very definite.

When invited to a meal, the guest should offer a gift of flowers and the guest is often adorned with garlands of flowers. On such occasions, the flowers should be removed and carried in the hand as a sign of humility.

The people of India are very polite and expect the same in return. They are often too polite to say no to an invitation; if they cannot attend, they will more likely say "I'll try."

Indonesia

In Indonesia, never touch another person's head, for this is thought to be where the spirit resides. Although handshaking is becoming more accepted, avoid using your left hand to pass or receive anything, for it is considered unclean and will be taken as an insult.

Negotiating is crucial in Indonesia. However, never pressure or hurry, and be prepared to bargain.

In business punctuality is expected. Presenting your business card is essential to gaining respect and acknowledgment.

Iran

Iranians are polite and formal. If offered tea, you should drink it or at least sip it; don't ask for coffee unless offered some initially. You may be served fruit or cakes during the meeting; you should take one after your host has offered.

Most meetings will begin with an icebreaking personal conversation; in many instances it is considered rude to get down to business right away.

The exchanging of gifts is not uncommon in business dealings—which, after all, have a very significant personal element to them in Iran. Usually, pens, pins, books, or small souvenirs of either your company or of your country are appreciated. The most senior person should always receive the nicest gift.

Ireland

The Irish toast their visitors, and consider refusal to drink a bit of an insult. So if you must refuse, always say it's for health reasons. Make business appointments in advance; however, keep in mind that the Irish are not very time conscious. In Ireland the official language is Gaelic, but it is never used in business. Avoid discussing religion or politics.

When meeting the Irish, the proper greeting is to shake hands, extend a warm greeting, and maintain eye contact. Handshakes should also be exchanged upon departure.

When meeting a woman, a man should wait for her to extend her hand before offering his. When being introduced, make an effort to engage in immediate eye contact, and sustain it; when especially interested, the Irish will make an overt effort to do the same.

The distance between speakers is usually less than between other northern Europeans. However, the Irish tend to value their personal space and will expect the same of you.

If you speak in an animated manner, tone down your hand gestures. It is highly regarded to maintain a conservative demeanor in personal and professional contexts.

Gestures have a lot of significance. Pointing is accomplished by using the chin, rather than the fingers. Touching one's nose is a sign of confidentiality. Use the index finger to indicate the number one and the thumb for number five. The peace sign or "V" made by extending the index and middle finger with the palm facing out, is an obscene gesture in Ireland and should be avoided.

Avoid the North American expression "Have a nice day;" it comes across as sounding questionable.

Italy

Generally, Italians prefer third-party introductions whenever possible. You will be introduced to the older people and women first. Moreover, when introducing yourself, follow this protocol.

Upon introductions and departures, shake hands with everyone individually in a group—a group wave is not appreciated. Frequent warm and vigorous handshakes can be common for both business and social occasions. Italians will not hesitate to greet people they know with an embrace.

Do not presume to seat yourself at a gathering; whenever possible, wait to be told where to sit. Meals in Italy are generally unhurried, and can last up to four hours. During the meal, it is impolite to put your hands in your lap. At the table, it is also impolite to stretch.

Italians are often animated and like to gesture with their hands. Placing the hand on the stomach signifies dislike, usually for another person. Rubbing the chin with the fingertips, and then propelling them forward, is a gesture of contempt. Contorting the fingers and hand to resemble the devil's horns pointed outward is an obscene gesture. Pointing the fingers inward, however, is a sign to ward off evil. Pointing with the index and little finger is a gesture used only when wishing someone bad luck. Whenever, possible avoid raising your hand or fingers.

Slapping one's raised arm above the elbow and thumbing the nose are both considered extremely offensive.

In public, behavior such as chewing gum, leaning, and slouching are unacceptable.

Japan

In Japan manners are a form of showing great respect. Avoid excessive physical and eye contact and backslapping. Do not point directly at someone with your finger or shout loudly to get someone's attention.

Appearance is important and it is offensive to wear tattered clothes outside. Avoid wearing slippers into a straw-mat room or into the entrance to a home where the shoes are kept outside.

The entire family uses the same bath water. As a guest, you will probably be offered the bath water first. When you are finished, do not drain the tub.

While in public view or in formal situations, do not chew gum. It is impolite to eat or drink something while walking down the street.

Do not bite or clean your fingernails, gnaw on pencils, or lick your fingers in front of others.

When eating with others, it is impolite to pour

your own drink—pour your companion's drink and your companion pours yours. If you do not want any more to drink, leave your glass full.

When eating out, do not make excessive special requests in the preparation of your food or wolf it down. Do not put soy sauce on your rice; it is not meant for that. It is normal to make slurping sounds when eating noodles.

Do not use your chopsticks to skewer food, move dishes around, and never dish out food to another using the same end of the chopsticks you just ate from. Do not use chopsticks to point at someone. Do not leave your chopsticks standing up out of your food.

It is normal to pay a restaurant or bar bill at the register, rather than giving money to the waiter or waitress; there is no tipping.

Poland

When dealing with business associates in Poland, don't use a person's first name until they do. The Polish consider using first names a sign of friendship, and often celebrate this event over a drink. If you are a woman, don't be surprised if the men kiss your hand each time you meet.

Coffee is in very short supply, so unless it is served, don't ask for it. When a Pole flicks his finger against his neck, he is inviting you to join him for a drink of vodka.

Russia

When meeting, Russians shake hands firmly. Pointing with the index finger is considered impolite, but it is frequently done. Russians enjoy giving and receiving gifts. Although not expected, guests usually bring the host a gift of flowers, food, or vodka. If bringing flowers, be certain the number of flowers is uneven—even-numbered flowers are for funerals.

When entering a home, prepare to remove your shoes. You may be given a pair of slippers to wear. Do not shake hands or kiss across the threshold this is traditionally bad luck.

Russians prefer to have social interaction before discussing business. Doing business over the telephone without meeting the prospective client or partner is ineffective.

Check your coat, briefcase, or parcels at the door of a restaurant, theater, or any formal reception.

For business travelers, be certain to have plenty of business cards—one side printed in English, the other in Russian.

Offer to share your snacks and cigarettes with those around you, especially on the train or at an office. Be prepared to accept smoking. Be prepared to accept all alcohol and food offered when visiting friends, and it can be quite a lot. Refusing a drink or a toast is a serious breach of etiquette. An open bottle must often be finished.

Business people dress conservatively with good shoes. Men should not remove their jackets without asking. Women should cover their heads with a scarf or hat in Russian Orthodox Churches.

When with a man, women should not be assertive in public, carry heavy bags, open doors, or uncork bottles. They also should not pay for themselves in social situations.

Saudi Arabia

Once in this country, be aware you are no longer under the protection of your home country. You are subject to Saudi Islamic law, so study the laws well.

When visiting a business colleague in Saudi Arabia, do not be startled if he holds your hand while you walk. This is simply a sign of friendship.

In addition, when you arrive for an appointment, remember that other business people may be present and that several meetings may be happening simultaneously.

When a veiled Saudi woman is with a Saudi man, it is not customary for her to be introduced. Arab women in public places are expected to wear a veil to make themselves invisible. Women business travelers will be accepted without veils, but only if they dress conservatively. It is wise, however, to have a scarf on hand.

Foreign women may go shopping and travel

alone; however, they should avoid the all-male cafes. All women are not allowed to drive.

Saudi men often walk hand in hand. If a Saudi holds your hand, accept this gesture of friendship. The left hand is considered unclean—always use the right hand. Moreover, avoid gesturing with the left hand. Pointing is rude and the "thumbs up" sign is offensive throughout the Arab world.

Ask permission before taking photographs of other people.

Saudis have great respect for the religious written word. Do not wrap anything in an Arabic-language newspaper, since it may contain Allah's name. Moreover, a copy of the Koran must be handled with tremendous care and respect.

Scotland

When in Scotland, refer to the people as "Scots" or "Scotsmen." The word "Scotch" refers only to a drink. Never call a kilt a skirt, and avoid making jokes about this formal Scottish attire, which is often worn by both men and women.

The Scots tend to be reserved people; handshakes are generally light, and hugging is not common, even among close friends. Scots tend to be a low-contact people. Rather than touching or getting too close, it is more appropriate to maintain at least one arm's length distance from your Scottish counterpart.

Make an effort to speak in a low, moderate tone of voice. Talking too loudly in public is sometimes considered offensive and embarrassing. In conversation. The Scots tend to downplay hand gestures and other physical expressions.

Singapore

Singapore is a city-state; there are no rural areas and no other cities. The official languages are Malay, Chinese, Tamil, and English. Singaporeans have a strong work ethic. It is considered impolite for the bottom of the foot to point to someone. Touching another person's head is also impolite.

Singapore has strict laws carrying heavy fines for littering, spitting, and chewing gum; and smoking is banned in most public places. Laws regarding jaywalking or drug enforcement are strictly enforced. It is wise for foreigners to carry prescriptions for all medications to avoid trouble with the authorities.

A handshake, followed by an exchange of business cards is the usual greeting in Singapore. Many in the commercial sector follow a relaxed Western approach to business; however, a few traditionalists remain who will expect a show of deference on first meeting and will then return the courtesy. Punctuality is seen as a mark of respect to the host at business and social gatherings.

Tipping is not usual in Singapore, although it is becoming more prevalent. The more expensive restaurants and hotels add a ten percent service charge and may actively discourage any additional gratuity; but if none is added, leave ten percent. Service personnel in the larger hotels can be offered money for good service and taxi fares should be rounded up to the nearest dollar. Tipping is prohibited at the airport.

When visiting a mosque or temple in Singapore, appropriate clothing should be worn as a sign of respect. All the island's main religions request the removal of shoes before entering.

Spain

A wide variety of gestures regularly accompany conversation. Do not hesitate to ask if you have difficulty understanding gestures, especially since the meanings vary from region to region. Spaniards get a sense of identity from their particular region rather than the country as a whole. Be sensitive to regional differences.

When summoning someone, turn your palm down, then wave the fingers on your entire hand. One common gesture is snapping the hands downward to emphasize a point. The North American "O.K." symbol (making a circle of the index finger and the thumb) is considered vulgar. Spain is a highly religious country, and many are offended when one takes the Lord's name in vain. Refrain from any type of swearing in the presence of others.

Thailand

Respect in Thailand is important, especially for monks. When introduced to a monk, never touch him; a verbal greeting will suffice. Women should never touch a monk or hand him an object directly. The back seat of a bus is reserved for monks. When you are on a bus or train and see a monk standing, offer him your seat.

Never walk in front of Thais praying in a temple. Touching a Buddha is perceived only as a sign of disrespect. When walking into a room where a Buddha image is found, be certain to step over the threshold rather than walking on it; it is believed that souls live there.

Before entering a Buddhist temple, hats and shoes must be removed. Articles left outside the temple have been known to be stolen. It is suggested one wear old and inexpensive footwear and hats to reduce the likelihood of theft.

In a theater or auditorium, the front row is reserved for monks and high-ranking officials. People of lesser rank sit behind them, based of the rank and file of the people present.

The monarch should always be respected. Consequently, never put Thai banknotes in your shoes, socks, or other questionable places. Also, be certain to stand as a sign of respect when the Thai national anthem is playing.

It is considered rude to point at anyone with your foot. Crossing our legs is considered inappropriate seating. The proper way to sit is to kneel with your legs tucked underneath your body as you face the person of honor.

Thais tend to smile constantly. This is not always an indication of amusement. Often a smile is to mask embarrassment, nervousness, or disapproval.

Etiquette
Today

Current Etiquette

The argument has raged for many years that actually there are no manners anymore and that society is becoming more ill-mannered and boorish with each generation. We do not favor a return to the courts of France and the powdered wigs and silk stockings for men or a submissive and superficial role for women. However, there must be a middle ground of good taste in dress, speech, table etiquette, public comportment, and general respect that is preferable to the shapeless, selfish, and thoughtless direction of late.

Let me discuss the rules of behavior still believed to be important, along with some new ideas for the age in which we currently live.

Manners in Everyday Life

Good manners and etiquette are not complicated and are generally patterned on courtesy and an attitude of kindness and consideration for others.

With just the most basic idea of decent behavior, anyone can conduct himself or herself better in social or personal situations. Add to this attitude some basic rules and one becomes a person of good manners and simple social skills.

No one is born knowing the rules of etiquette. Some seem to pick up the nicer points of social conduct faster than others; however, anyone who is even moderately observant can learn the rules of etiquette in almost any situation. These rules are learned gradually in the home, at school, at work, and in our social situations. There are courses that can be taken; however, to truly know and use these rules, one must practice them as a habit of daily living and make them a part of his or her personality.

People have different reasons for wanting to learn good manners. Consider how you would like to be treated, and what others do to make you feel the most comfortable. If you will notice, people with manners or knowledge of handling themselves in public or social situations make friends more easily. When people are kind and sympathetic to others, they naturally become more popular and are considered better companions.

Good manners are important at home and in public. Treating family members with respect and consideration usually equates to similar behavior in public. Good manners also help you with members of the families of friends, special friends, employers, teachers, and people with whom you come in contact daily, such as sales people, and police officers. Good manners, opposed to bad manners, put others at ease, and make them more cooperative.

On the other hand, not knowing what to do and being uncomfortable in social situations can make a potentially exciting evening or event very awkward and unpleasant. If you are not aware of rules of speech or table manners, or other behavior patterns, you will have a limited social life and your self-esteem can take a real beating.

In a job or working situations, you can show the respect of good manners by showing up on time, by being reliable, by personal grooming, and by respecting others' ideas and space. Simple things like turning in assignments on time, and having them well prepared and neat, can show respect for an employer or teacher and are considered good etiquette. Not showing off and having respect for other people's property are also signs of good manners in public.

In addition, a well-mannered employee also keeps those confidential items truly confidential, can be trusted, and is helpful to others. To carry the daily work etiquette one step further is the workplace social situation. Examples include: knowing how to make an introduction, how to order from a menu, how to set a buffet table, and how much and to whom you should pay a tip or gratuity.

You may, from time to time, find yourself in an unfamiliar situation for which there seems to be no rule. In these situations, it becomes the responsibility of the individual to show common sense and good judgement in deciding what behavior is appropriate. Many times, common sense and good judgement come from watching and learning from others who exhibit these qualities.

Male Courtesies

Traditional male courtesies reflect a sincere feeling of concern and caring. It is still proper for a man to open the car door for a lady. However, there has been more than a suggestion lately that these courtesies are too chauvinistic and even offensive to some. If you fear that what you observe as a courtesy may be misinterpreted, simply ask the lady if she wishes these courtesies or not.

Many of these acts are still quite practical. Getting into or out of a low car can be a little difficult when wearing a skirt, without a small assist. The gentleman need only offer his hand, palm up, to the lady to help her into or out of the car. If it is a larger vehicle or a bus, you may gently support or take hold of her elbow. When arriving at the door, the gentleman still holds the door open, or if there is a doorman, steps back to let the lady enter first.

How to Treat a Lady

If this is a first date or encounter with a lady, the first step is to find out how she wishes to be treated. It may, of course, depend upon the place and the situation to a great degree. While most of us do not change clothes four times a day and go from brunch to polo to the governor's ball, the place and the occasion do make a difference.

Learn to communicate. Find out something about your date. Where has she lived? What is her education level? What are her interests? What are her expectations?

Respect her. If you have asked a lady to spend some time with you, whether at the bowling alley or the symphony, the basic rules of respect still apply. You may want to find out how she feels about your paying her way or "going Dutch," if she wishes the traditional male/female manners applied (opening the car door, assisting her with her chair at dinner, etc.), or if she feels more comfortable as a peer.

Basic respect also involves your speech. Avoid being loud and boisterous (unless she has already accepted you as that). Avoid condescension, or acting as if you know it all and she knows nothing.

Talk about subjects that interest her. Do not interrupt her. Be careful about humor. Avoid off-colored stories or jokes that diminish someone else. Do not ignore her or appear aloof and superior.

Talk "to" her rather than "at" her. Assume that she is intelligent and carry on an open and interesting conversation. In the interest of relationships, a good open conversation can lead to a very enjoyable evening and breaks down barriers.

Be yourself in the conversation. Even if you are simply dying to make a good impression with her, avoid making the wrong one by seeming to be what you are not, or putting on manners that will eventually wear off. If the cravat and cigarette holder approach is not really you, do not try it.

Keep your hands to yourself. This may be very difficult, but it is to your benefit. The lady needs to feel comfortable with you and not as if she must defend herself from the moment you meet. Generally, small touches and other ways of showing affection will happen quite naturally and she will give signals about her acceptance or rejection of the idea. Do not push it. By being casual and respectively physical, you will be more appealing to her.

Tell her you enjoy her company. There will be opportune times during the course of the date for you to express the fact that you are honestly having a good time.

If you are not, simply obey the other rules, continue to treat her as a lady and do not call again. However, even if it is not the romantic interlude you dreamed of, when you leave her at her door, thank her for spending the evening with you. You may not have been any more exciting to her than she to you, but you can still both be courteous.

How to Be a Lady

I recall a casual date I had at a very transitional time in my life. A friend had arranged for me to have dinner with a young lady I had never met. She was going away to school the next day and I was to report for a prior commitment with Uncle Sam. Neither of us had any romantic fantasies or expectations for any kind of relationship.

This was not the most attractive young woman I had ever dated; in fact, she could have been called "plain." The evening turned out to be one of the most pleasant I had spent in a long time. The usual boy/girl games were absent and the lady was absolutely charming. She was intelligent and had the grace and comfort that comes with good manners and honest conversation.

That was the night I learned to appreciate "plain," grace, and poise. I don't even remember the young lady's name, but I remember her manners and grace—that was forty-one years ago.

The Victorian ideals are not necessarily old-fashioned when it comes to being a lady. Poise, charm, and a certain detachment are quite appealing. If a lady is to develop any of what is sometimes called a "mystique," she has a better chance through her manners and her graciousness than through any physical attribute.

Learn a quiet confidence. In a world growing more outlandish all the time, to be quietly apart from the din and clatter is again to be very appealing. To be confident in manner and in manners is not, however, something you just "put on." This type of attitude and demeanor requires some study, a lot of observing of those who have mastered this graceful position in life, and a fair amount of study in a lot of varying areas, so that the quiet confidence is real and a part of your personality.

Dress modestly and tastefully. I will cover this aspect more in subsequent chapters. The idea of both modesty and taste may be subject to debate; however, there are some rules or standards that have passed the test of time. Do not become a slave to fads. You will find that fad and fashion are not the same. Avoid extreme clothing or makeup that only serves to draw attention but does not leave the right kind of message. Select clothing that suits you.

We all have a certain number of imperfections to live with or to attempt to cover; it may be height or the lack of it. It may be weight, or it may be something else that we perceive to be a flaw. Only the best of figures or physiques can survive leggings or muscle shirts. Avoid very tight clothing or very revealing clothing.

Makeup is meant to enhance not to overpower. An understatement is far preferable to an overstatement. Select subtle colors of makeup that enhance or flatter you rather than those that simply "add a coat of paint."

Speak like a lady. In my brief summary of a lady

before I get into the details, nothing can be more frequently urged upon a woman, young or old, who wishes to be thought a lady, than the reminder to talk like one.

It seems that we are currently of a mentality where many women believe or would like others to believe that to compete or be thought "equal" in a man's world, they must talk like a deckhand or a sailor on leave. If you want to get someone's attention—man or woman—speak politely, speak without bluster or brass, and avoid all the more popular four letter words and references to bodily functions or parts. An intelligent and soft-spoken lady is extremely attractive and also the match for anyone in a social or professional situation.

Do not, on the other hand, spew a lot of ten-dollar words that confuse more than impress. Furthermore, if you do not use such words correctly, it can be quite embarrassing.

You need not be shy about entering into any

conversation where you feel comfortable; there are few subjects these days that are not considered open to ladies. Even here, however, it may be more how you do this than what you do.

If you have developed that air of class and poise, you will always conduct yourself accordingly and will know what conversational topics you may wish to politely avoid. I am not necessarily an advocate of complete "political correctness," as it is often far too superficial and meaningless, but being careful is always a good idea.

Women's Apparel

I discovered some timeless advice in a book of etiquette by one of the very precise and proper experts that is still worth considering, although this advice was written some forty years ago. The sizes and shapes of people have not changed in that time. Neither have the struggles most of us endure to look good in the less than perfect state in which we find ourselves. Please take the following information, which I have borrowed, as you will.

• Short Women—Most of this information can apply to men at one time or another; however, women are usually more aware of their appearance and their choices in social situations.

Short women should choose clothes with a long vertical line rather than something that looks horizontal. Avoid wide belts, horizontal patterns, and large prints. Higher heels on shoes may help, but not if the heel is too tall, making it difficult to walk gracefully. Hair that can be piled up on the head may help. Avoid turtleneck sweaters, heavy but short necklaces, and large earrings.

• Tall Women—Of course, just the opposite is true for the tall and lean person. Avoid the vertical stripes that accentuate the height and use belts or two-piece outfits to moderate the look. The tall person can wear contrasting colors in jacket and skirt, skirt and blouse, or sweater and slacks. The tall girl can find shoes with a lower heel and should avoid the taller hairdo's.

• Sturdy Women—A large but dear friend of mine once insisted that I refer to him as a "thick" person. Whatever the descriptive wording, there are some cautions in selecting a wardrobe. The lady who is inclined to be a little plump is similar to the very short person. She should avoid large prints, wide belts, heavy or bulky materials, and tight-fitting clothing. Fortunately there are stores now that cater to the larger or "queen" size lady and there are people who will advise on clothing that looks more becoming. Large or baggy clothes do not help, but there are items with an "A" line and not gathered at the waist that are quite becoming. Big women can still be very attractive if they take some time and good advice about what they wear.

In selecting shoes, the heavy person usually has to give a lot of consideration to comfort. But, again, avoid very high heels for comfort and balance. As far as swimsuits and shorts, for the most part they are out of the picture.

• The Average Figure—If you are a lady of average figure, you will have some strong points and some weak points. The idea is simply to accentuate the positive and eliminate the negative. Choose colors and styles that will do just that. Light colors make you or your hips look larger, dark colors are more flattering and hide more. Evaluate your assets ladies and see if you really should wear the stirrup pants and the shorts, or whether you should opt for something that is less telling. If age has begun to creep up on you, reconsider the look of sleeveless blouses, halter tops and very tight jeans.

• Vulgar Attire—Vulgarity is a term that dates itself and does not necessarily refer to sexuality. In the times when manners were considered Victorian, to be vulgar referred to poor speech, clothes that were gaudy or loud, and jewelry that was flashy. It also referred to necklines that were too low and skirts or sweaters that were too tight— any attire drawing undue attention.

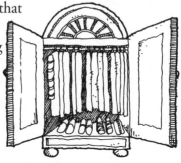

How to Be a Gentleman

In today's world, especially, many of the same rules apply that I have discussed with the ladies. However, a man's conduct really does hark back more specifically to the days of chivalry and the code of the knights. While there will always be a few who will feel that Brando's role in "A Streetcar Named Desire," was a gentlemanly example, I would recommend that you follow more closely Cary Grant or David Niven.

While reciting the attributes of a gentleman does not exactly read like the promises of a boy scout, it may be closer than you think. Going back to the British idea of the country gentleman as opposed to the French courtesan, there is the ideal of some deeper character than just another pretty face and glib tongue.

A true gentleman is trustworthy, of good report, kind to women, gentle and patient with children, fair-minded, honest, temperate, and soft-spoken.

A gentleman is also cautious in his speech, not given to coarse talk or off-colored stories (especially in the presence of ladies), not a braggart, slow to anger, and not given to outbursts of violence.

When it comes to mannerly behavior, many men fail in two basic places: at the table and in conversation. If you are really interested in acceptable behavior, these are two areas where you are being watched very closely. Even the most modest mother has her own ideas of how a man should behave and how he should speak.

As for eating, the basics are: do not slurp your soup (except in Japan), keep your elbows off the table, take small bites, do not belch or pick your teeth. Eat slowly, and allow a little polite conversation into the meal, but do not talk with food in your mouth. Do not eat off your guest's plate and do not see how much food you can consume in a given amount of time.

Relax—this really is a social time. There will be occasions when you think you are absolutely starving and the food in front of you is seemingly more important than the air you breathe. However, when you are at a social meal or on a date, this is the time to be polite, not rushed, and get the most out of the company. You, of course, can enjoy your meal and it may become a part of the conversation, but it is only part of the reason you are there.

Most men are incredibly bad listeners, which, if you did not know, is an important part of conversation. If you are interested in the business meeting, the social lunch, or the first meeting with someone, you must learn to listen. It is good sense; you will learn something by being a good listener. You will also make other people feel better and more important, which is a basic reason for good manners. Finally, by listening you may be perceived as being intelligent, thoughtful, and sophisticated.

When beginning a conversation, always direct it

to someone else in the room—whether a date, spouse, a new acquaintance, or whomever, but not toward yourself. Speak of yourself and your marvelous accomplishments when asked, but do not embellish or take advantage of the situation to boast upon yourself.

The ancient Greeks did not think modesty to be necessary or particularly important; the perfect Greek was very interested in himself. The Romans, on the other hand, thought modesty to be a great virtue and valued the man who presented himself in noble deeds rather than embellished speeches.

Be positive—even if you do not feel that way when in a social situation. Nothing will dampen an event or end a social evening faster than someone who is constantly complaining or whining, especially about personal relationships such as friends, employers, or spouses. This is a very good way to ensure you are not invited back.

You should also avoid topics like politics and

religion. If strong feelings exist, you may want to be careful about some sports issues or figures.

In summary, a gentleman always considers the feelings of others, the situation, the culture, and the circumstance in his conversational behavior. In most social situations, you do not wish the conversation to get out of hand, or to become argumentative or heated; it is the responsibility of a gentleman to see that this does not happen. Keep it light and open if it is purely a social situation.

Good Grooming

Good grooming refers more to the person than the clothing, yet it has something to do with fashion. Mostly, however, this refers to you.

Here are the rudiments of grooming: brush your teeth, wash your hands before eating and after using the bathroom, comb or arrange your hair, keep your hair washed and clean, and bathe or shower with great regularity.

At one time, good grooming had more to do with a person's clothing than it may appear to have today. However, when in social circles or in a professional or business setting, even casual may have a different meaning.

We must admit that every generation has chosen styles of its own that seem quite puzzling to the previous generation. This includes hair, clothing, music, speech, and forms of entertainment. Dirty and unkempt was never fashionable and will never be acceptable.

As I mentioned with hair, regardless of the style, to be acceptable, hair must be clean and show some attempt at having been arranged. Even with today's spikes, wild colors, and head shaving, cleanliness is still important.

The same applies to clothing. Here, also, each generation chooses styles quite their own. I recall when girls wore several petticoats under wide skirts of felt or wool. The young ladies spent hours getting these rigs ready with starch or sugar solutions to make them stiff. It was nearly impossible for them to get into a school desk or under the steering wheel of the family car.

Later, the miniskirt came in and signaled one of

the cardinal rules of dress etiquette: every fashion is not appropriate for everybody. Even if it is the style and everybody is wearing a muscle shirt, if you look puny and ghastly in one, it is not right for you.

Family and friends should counsel a teenage girl who desperately wants to wear a miniskirt, but looks like ten pounds of potatoes stuffed into a five-pound bag.

As I have said before, the well-groomed and classy person will wear what suits him or her, not just what is in fashion at the time. Now, having said that, it still is true that some order, some color coordination, and care with the condition of the clothing are all still important.

Greetings

I will begin this discussion with two areas that seem to be rather crippled, if not completely dead yet: greetings and conversation. The art of greetings covers a large area.

Greetings are both spoken and written and run the gamut from informal and casual to the most specific way to greet by title. The simplest form of greeting is when you meet someone and simply acknowledge him or her. Even if it is the norm in most parts of the country now, "Hi," is not an acceptable greeting. Especially in a first meeting, "Hello," or "How do you do?" or "Pleased to meet you," are much more pleasant and literate.

When introducing someone say, "I would like you to meet . . ." or "May I introduce . . ." or in a less formal but still acceptable way "This is . . ." A man should always stand (and usually a woman) when being introduced to someone else.

Gift Protocol

Gifts are given for many reasons, but there is a certain etiquette to each event. The most common are holiday gifts. It is awkward when having to buy for coworkers and others you do not know well. It is appropriate to buy a holiday gift for your boss if:

- you work in a small office.

- you work closely with your boss.

- you buy in a group from everyone.

- you are invited to his or her home for a party.

You may choose to purchase something for your child's teacher. Some appropriate gifts include a book, a journal, a golden apple, a silver apple, a basket of fruit, or fresh flower arrangements. Keep the gifts impersonal to eliminate any misunderstanding of intent.

• Christmas (or Chanukah) gifts for a hostess—
are appreciated at a holiday party and may include
a plant or fresh flowers, an ornament in good
taste, a box of chocolates, a crystal or silver candy
dish, or wine—let your budget and the type of
party be your guide.

• Christmas (or Chanukah) gifts for someone
who stops by unexpectedly—may include a
decorated jar of jam, a poinsettia, or a box of
chocolates. Of course, you are under no obligation
to reciprocate.

• Christmas/gifts for a coworker—depend on the
office environment. If your office is in the habit of
exchanging gifts, ask around discretely to get an
idea of expectations. Often it's a white elephant
exchange and a box of candy or an ornament will
suffice.

• Hostess gifts—are in good taste when invited to
a party or dinner—a bottle of wine, chocolates,

flowers in a vase, etc. The gift can be delivered earlier or later than the event. Flowers can be sent the next day as a thank you for the evening.

• Birth gifts—are appropriate should you visit the mother and child in the hospital, even if you have already bestowed one at an earlier shower. This gift needn't be extravagant—a potted plant, flowers, a receiving blanket, or booties, etc.

• Christenings/Baptismal gifts—are taken only if there is a reception. If the affair is held during church service with no reception to follow, no gift is necessary. A grandmother typically provides the christening gown. This is no requirement, merely a nice tradition with many.

• Engagement gifts—are bestowed only by the intended to his bride-to-be or vice versa. Typically a guest does not know it is an engagement party, so they consider bringing only the traditional hostess gift.

• Graduation gifts—(from other than the parents, Godparents, and grandparents) should be small tokens of esteem. Since only family and exceptionally close friends should be invited to such an affair, you are under no obligation to send a gift to the graduate. If you wish to keep on good terms with someone, a card is a nice gesture.

• Housewarming gifts—are common at a housewarming party. Something that is appropriate to a new house—a plant, a vase, a bottle of wine, etc.

• Elopement gifts—are taken only if the bride decides to have a reception. If no party commemorates this occasion, you may keep or return the gift, or give it to her anyway, with best wishes.

• Commitment gifts—are for a gay couple who are committing to each other. This is considered a wedding and addressed in the same manner.

• Shower gifts—are recommended, even if you are

not attending. If you are invited to more than one shower for the same person, you are not required to bring a gift to each; however, bear in mind that you may hurt feelings if you don't.

You must also consider who the gifts are for. At a baby shower, it is traditionally for the baby, but what new mother wouldn't appreciate something for herself.

At a bridal shower, the gifts are for the bride alone. This is a way for the bride to increase her trousseau or her hope chest.

If you are being invited to the shower, but not the wedding, it is within your rights to not attend the shower—unless it is an extremely small (family only) wedding; then you should attend the shower and wish the bride well.

• Wedding gifts—are to be considered a separate gift from the wedding shower. The gift at the shower was for the bride. The gift at the wedding is for the couple.

If you are not attending the wedding, you are not obligated to send a gift; however, many will expect it. If you are not well known to the couple, a card would suffice. A check or cash is an appropriate gift and often greatly appreciated. Many expect you to bring a gift of the $80 to $150 range, if the wedding is a fancy expensive affair.

If you do not know the bride or groom well, find out where they are registered and purchase something they have suggested. The registration is merely to assist those who can't think of an appropriate gift.

When arriving from out of town, your gift to the couple is your attendance; however, a gift of another sort will likely be expected.

Anniversary gifts—

Year	Traditional Gift	Modern Gift
1st year	Paper	Clocks
2nd year	Cotton	China
3rd year	Leather	Crystal/Glass
4th year	Linen/Silk	Electric Appliances
5th year	Wood	Silverware
6th year	Iron	Wood
7th year	Wool/Copper	Desk Sets
8th year	Bronze	Linens/laces
9th year	Pottery/China	Leather
10th year	Tin/Aluminum	Diamond Jewelry
11th year	Steel	Jewelry/Accessories
12th year	Silk	Pearls/Gems
13th year	Lace	Textiles/Furs
14th year	Ivory	Gold/Jewelry
15th year	Crystal	Watches
20th year	China	Platinum
25th year	Silver	Sterling Silver
30th year	Pearl	Diamond
35th year	Coral	Jade
40th year	Ruby	Ruby
45th year	Sapphire	Sapphire
50th year	Gold	Gold
55th year	Emerald	Emerald
60th year	Diamond	Diamond

Manners
at Home

Manners in the Home

Now that I have covered the basics for those who want to learn the way to behave during a date or appointment, let me begin the detail of etiquette at the beginning. What manners do you learn or understand while growing up that will serve you well in your adult life?

Emily Post, who was hailed as a queen of polite society, specifically addressed the manners in the home and family life.

Emily Post remarked that she was often asked for suggestions on teaching etiquette to children or young adults and also whether she felt there were any special rules in teaching manners to the young. In a reasonable response, she referred to the need to teach by being an example to the young and incorporating consistency and firmness. The most important part of this message, of course, is example.

Very simply, if good manners and grace are a part

of the home on a daily basis, they will be learned. If shoved upon a child as the way to behave "out in public," they may just backfire at the most embarrassing times.

This now becomes something of a discussion on parenting skills and success, as well as manners. If a child is patiently taught in an adult manner the use of social skills, table manners, politeness to adults, etc., those attitudes will remain.

If they are not taught, the breaking of bad habits at a later date or amending bad manners and behavior can be a real challenge, to say the least.

Manners, as in the days of chivalry (which we choose to believe is not dead), were also a matter of convictions and standards. It is well to discuss this behavioral idea with children as we teach them manners, or they can develop into some very sweet, courteous, little monsters.

Within their world, children can be taught manners as a matter of daily course. This equates to ideas like fair play, sharing, and polite conversation. Here is the children's equivalent of what I described as a lady or a gentleman. Children can, indeed, be taught to appreciate fairness, respect the property of others, and not to be too boastful about themselves.

There is a real skill here also in teaching a child how to deal with success and failure, and to accept both with a generous and graceful manner. It is important to know how to receive the trophy for first place, but it is also important to know how to congratulate the person who just defeated you in an important competition.

Dignity will always be an important part of manners and etiquette. We see in our minds some old movie, probably European, where the hero or heroine bravely steps up to accept some horrible circumstance or disappointment with a quiet and uncomplaining courage. This kind of dignity and grace are taught to us as children. In the end, not all children will behave commendably in a dreadful situation; however, we can still teach them how to accept the defeat that will surely come.

One of the most difficult situations that a parent has to overcome in teaching behavioral patterns to children is the excuse, "well, everyone else does it." Most children and adults will follow the customs of the community, and in most cases should be allowed to do so. But there are also some exceptions here that parents must consider.

Bad manners and selfish or bullying behavior mixed with crude language need not be accepted regardless of the community standards.

Parents make these choices for their children to be different at some degree of risk. Sometimes the risk is clearly worth taking. I remember that my mother always insisted I had on clean clothes and my hair combed whenever I left the house, even to play in the vacant fields that surrounded our new housing development. One time, over my loud protests, she dressed me up in a little sailor suit, slicked back my hair and sent me out with the neighbor kids. Of course, I got my designer outfit dirty crawling around in the dirt making roads and forts and the like.

The real damage was done, however, when one particularly aggressive boy taunted me about my classy attire. It ended up in a fight with both of us rolling around on the ground and throwing poorly aimed and not very damaging punches.

Clearly there could have been some middle ground here where my mother's ideas of cleanliness could have presented me to my present community in a less dangerous condition.

Acceptable Eating Habits

There will be some repetition in this volume, but generally only where I deem it necessary and acceptable. Repeated discussions of table manners, especially with young people these days, are most permissible. The dinner table, and to a lesser degree the breakfast table, should be a place of learning in most homes. As a place to learn many things about the world, not only manners, the family meal, enjoyed together and with some regularity and structure, is irreplaceable. Of course, there must be rules about how you behave at the dining table.

- Be clean and neat when you come to the table.

- Chew quietly with your mouth closed.

- Do not overload your fork.

- Do not play with your food.

- Learn the proper way to use eating utensils.

- Do not interrupt adults, but see that children are included in family conversations.

- If finished before others, ask to be excused before leaving the table.

The parents' responsibility is to make it possible and comfortable for the young child to keep all the rules that are assigned at the table. The parents, in including the children in the conversation, should direct questions to them that are of interest and of which they have some knowledge.

The child should be congratulated and encouraged when the behavior is good, but handled gently and corrected with patience when there are improvements to be made. Making a battleground of mealtime will certainly defeat any attempt at teaching gentleness and good manners.

Additionally, the implements should be the right size and not too heavy, so as to allow the child to eat comfortably.

Some food may be cut into small bites so the young child can easily put it into his or her mouth without difficulty. The plate should not be piled too high or the portions be too large. The main purpose of mealtime may be nourishment, but it also needs to be a pleasant time and a place to learn and communicate.

Children's Appearance

It is important what children wear and when they begin to have a say in what they wear, it is important how to influence them. There are different schools of thought about selecting a child's clothing. Some people still feel that until well into the teens, all the clothing should be selected carefully by the parent.

Others feel that part of the growing and learning process is allowing a child to share in this activity and take the opportunity to teach what is preferable for certain occasions.

Some families tie this activity to allowances or when children begin to earn money around the house. When children begin to sense some financial power and independence, one of the first activities that they wish to participate in is the selection of clothing. By doing some teaching early on this matter, the child will learn something of independence as well as what is suitable. Additionally, the child will also learn to trust the parent in the selection of clothing.

The ultimate choice is still with the parent. The choice of play clothes is a good place to begin. A child and his or her experimentation can still be guided so you do not end up with disasters at the last minute before important events.

There are some pitfalls to avoid, although most mothers still make them at some time and learn painful lessons.

Do not overdress your child. If he or she is going to a party, call the parent of the child hosting the party to find what is appropriate. If it is a barbecue, don't send your little girl in lace and frills and your son in a tie and jacket. School clothes should also conform somewhat to those of the other children.

Never dress your child in clothes that are too old for them. I know a young man who was dressed in a full suit for church from the time he was about ten. The poor kid was terribly uncomfortable, and he took some unnecessary ribbing from the other boys. A suit at his age really was not necessary. I have also seen young girls struggle with heels and hose when they were simply not ready for them.

Conformity is important for children—often too important; however, there are reasonable ways to deal with this issue.

Applying Makeup

A little girl may be allowed to play with mom's lipstick in the house with some instruction to accompany this play. However, she should not be allowed to wear her own makeup until in her early teens. Young girls have such a natural and fresh look about them that makeup too early not only is unnecessary, but actually detracts from their beauty. Wearing makeup too young and on a continual basis can also be very bad for the skin and lead to other problems later on.

Most manner experts agree that nail polish and false fingernails can wait a long time. Young hands and activities are not conducive to the time beautiful fingernails need, and nails that are chipped or chewed are not attractive.

Teenager & Young Adult

Much has been said about the lack of good manners and basic respect among the young. This has been said in every age since the Romans and the Greeks. I do not necessarily agree that the youth of today are any worse than any other generation, but they get more media.

Young adults now begin to confront the issues of man/woman relationships, dating, tipping, etc. Young men and women of today do seem to mature faster and have the independence of mature adults at a younger age. This may be an advantage or a disadvantage as far as their etiquette and manners are concerned. There seem to be more coarse bad examples for them to view in what have always been customs for teenagers.

There are, nonetheless, more good examples if you just know where to go or to look. Good manners still, for the most part, begin at home and as I have already stated, begin with good examples and a lot of patience.

Just being strict about rules of etiquette is not always the best way. Many of us look back at some of the lessons we were taught and remember that many of them would have been easier if the teacher could simply hold off a little in the teaching.

Teaching the teenager may not be the nightmare some expect. None of us is too old to recall that we do not like being the subject of constant nagging.

For the teen, whose attention span and eagerness to learn manners may be underdeveloped, nagging is even more irritating. There will be times when you can get your teen's attention to discuss the fine points of etiquette. If you can do this and turn it into a fair and intelligent conversation, do not follow up your success with constant nagging.

You can do more good with gentle reminders such as notes, suggestions, setting out a tie or shirt, or helping with a place setting or invitation.

Telephone

Callers should identify themselves immediately. If they don't, you are correct to request the name of the caller before divulging if the person sought is home, busy, etc. When you have company and someone calls you, keep the call extremely brief with a promise to call back later.

It is polite to answer the phone with a simple "Hello." If you have a servant then adding the residents' name is not improper; however, remember that in these modern times the less information you give out to those you do not know, the better.

It is not impolite to hang up on telephone solicitors, after saying, "no thank you," and they continue.

It is impolite to call a residence after nine at night unless you have permission.

If you are calling to invite someone to an event, let them know that up front, rather than asking if they are available on a particular night. This keeps you from putting them in an awkward position.

Never forward a call to someone's residence without clearing this with them first.

When using call-waiting, remember that the first call is the priority. It is impolite to interrupt a conversation to take another call, especially more than once. If you have the call-waiting feature on your phone and you feel you must respond to a beep, do so quickly and graciously: "I have to answer this call. May I put you on hold for a second?" Then tell the other caller that you're in the middle of a conversation and arrange a time to get back to them. Return to the original person and finish your chat without rushing off.

If you are indeed expecting an important call, let the person on the other end know up front that there is a chance you might have to cut the conversation short.

Cellular Phone

Never use a cellular (cell) phone while driving unless it is "hands-free." Then be careful to limit conversations in cars to traffic areas and conditions requiring low amounts of decision making. If the conversation is important, pull over to the side of the road during the call.

Be careful to speak in hushed tones. A cell phone has a sensitive microphone capable of picking up a soft voice. Additionally, set the ring tone at a low level with a tune that is soft, gentle, and not annoying. The more crowded the situation, the quieter and softer the volume of voice and ring. When in situations such as church, a workshop, or a meeting where a ringing sound would prove disturbing to other people, use the vibrating feature.

Gain as little attention as possible. The goal is to communicate effectively without anyone else noticing or caring. Respect the personal space of other people and speak in places 10–20 feet or more away from the closest person. If there is no private, separate space available, wait to speak on the phone until a good space is available.

Keep business private. Many personal and business conversations contain information that should remain confidential or private. Before using a cell phone in a public location to discuss private business or issues, be certain there will be enough distance to keep the content private.

Keep a civil and pleasant tone. Others might overhear the conversation, so be careful to maintain a public voice that will not disturb others. Do not fire employees, chastise employees, argue with a boss or fight with a spouse or teenager on your cell phones in public settings.

Learn which spots offer the best signal and the best conditions to prevent holding an important business discussion or negotiation under poor conditions.

There are many situations where it would be rude if a phone rang, interrupting the transaction at hand. When stepping up to a service counter, entering a restaurant, or joining a meeting, turn off the phone and rely upon voice mail to take incoming calls.

Stepping to the counter to work out a problem with a ticket, the "cell-phone bore" takes an incoming call right in the middle of the transaction and holds up the employee as well as all the other customers lined up waiting for service. Oblivious to the inconvenience and inefficiency caused.

Teens & the Phone

Teens and telephones seem to have been made for each other, and also seem to create a unique etiquette and social problem. The common annoyance with teens is that they dominate the telephone and then express a great shock if someone suggests they limit their calls or that filling long periods of silence between two teens in different homes is not the best use of the device.

Young people need to understand what is acceptable and reasonable, but the lure of this device is also more than most teens can resist. As in other manners lessons, the phone should not be a bone of contention or an object of constant nagging.

It is not unreasonable to expect phone conversations to be of a moderate length when others are waiting; however, when there is plenty of time, the phone can be a very social and useful item.

When teens are growing into some degree of

social maturity, the phone is an island in the stream. Parents should try to understand how two friends can leave each other just for a few minutes and then desperately need a phone call.

As young people are growing into this social maturity, they also want some privacy in their telephone conversations, and should have it. Whether the teen is discussing a homework assignment with a classmate or the new boy down the street, the mannerly adult will grant them this. That being done, it is a far better chance that the teen will observe the manners requested by the parents.

It is appropriate for parents, however, to expect teens to observe rules about length of calls, times when others need the phone, and respect for the family schedule and needs.

While a teen with his or her own telephone and number enjoys a great status symbol and may relieve the parent, it should not be without rules. When feasible, the teen should pay the expenses of this separate phone. It is reasonable for the teen to be limited to the hours of use. Even with is or her own phone, the calls should be restricted at meal times, before everyone is awake in the morning, and after a reasonable hour in the evening.

There should be time for chores, study, and other events in which the family participates together when the teen's phone is not allowed to interrupt. If the teen does not answer the phone, the parents should not become message takers on that phone. Friends should understand they are not to call the parents' line to leave messages or find the teen.

Setting the Table

I will cover a formal dinner or table setting later; but first I will address the basics of setting a table. First, give some thought to the process and how you wish your table to look. In even the standard table setting, there is an element of design and presentation in addition to simply putting the utensils in the right place.

You will want matching place settings for everyone at the table. This includes plates, glasses, napkins, etc. Place mats and a tablecloth may or may not be used, depending on how informal you wish it to be. Also optional is a decorative centerpiece or some fresh flowers. All this should be in place at least a half hour before guests arrive.

Before you begin, even though everything will match, you want to take a little inventory to check what you have. Be certain everything is clean and ready to go.

Consider the tablecloth. Remember I am not talking about the formal dinner party yet, and within the bounds of good taste some creativity is in order. If you are using a tablecloth, be certain it is clean and pressed. Look for telltale stains from a previous party. The same is true of cloth napkins. This inspection should not be left to the last minute, lest some hurried cleaning or pressing is needed.

The standard table setting consists of a plate, flatware (knife, fork, and spoon), a water glass, and a napkin. You may add a coffee cup or serve the coffee separately later. Depending upon the menu, a separate bread plate or salad plate is appropriate. Even though this is not a formal setting, addressing the needs of the meal is necessary. There is a little more flexibility here than there used to be.

For a good-looking setup, the plate should be two inches in from the edge of the table; the fork to the left, placed on top of a folded napkin; the knife to the direct right of the plate with the cutting edge of the knife pointing in; and then the spoon on the outside. The handles of the flatware should be centered, and the drinking glass should be just above the plate and slightly to the right.

Now that everyone has a setting and all are in the right order, look to the creativity of your table. For formal settings, the tablecloth will be white; however, for less formal or buffet settings, you may wish to use a colored tablecloth. Floral-print bed sheets have occasionally been substituted for that touch of color. Here, too, is where you can add the floral centerpiece, another type of arrangement, or even fresh fruit or a combination to add some more color and distinction to the table. Your table decorations may suggest a particular theme—perhaps again in agreement with the menu, or simply to show some of your own personality.

Many occasions now call for something in-between the formal and standard setting where items are added for the convenience of the diner. If dessert is served as part of the setting, a dessert spoon should be added and should be laid at the top of the plate with the handle to the right.

Be prepared to adapt to your circumstances, such as seating the left-handed diner and accommodating menu items such as shrimp (shrimp fork), fondue (fondue fork), and a utensil to crack crab or lobster shells.

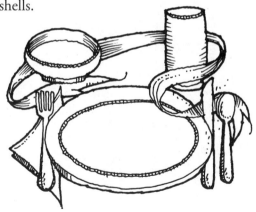

Dining Out Etiquette

Dining Out

Eating out at a restaurant can be a varied experience for young people. They will probably be very comfortable with the local fast-food places, and even the rib and chicken houses where you actually sit down to a table and use a knife and fork. However, I now move on to the occasion where they go to a nice place to dine and must be comfortable with not only the table setting but with themselves and their manners in public.

For many, the first public introduction to a formal table setting will be a nice restaurant surrounded with strangers. I sincerely hope the parents in these cases have taught the youth the basics of table etiquette and that they have a pleasant and comfortable evening without worrying about what to do with what particular part of the meal.

In the restaurant, you will be introduced to the courses of a meal and faced with the task of identifying the proper fork, spoon, glass, or plate.

When you order a full meal at a restaurant, it may include an appetizer, a drink, a salad, a bowl or cup of soup, a roll or sliced bread, the main course, dessert, and perhaps a cup of coffee or a cordial or other drink after the meal.

Whatever the dinner fare you order may be, keep one important rule in mind. Never make derogatory remarks or ungainly faces toward someone else's choice of food. However much you may dislike a dish, or question the edibility of an animal or vegetable, it is in the poorest taste to express these opinions and risk spoiling the enjoyment of a companion's meal.

Table Ready

When you are seated or soon after (some places set everything out, others bring items out with each course) you will see before you a neatly folded linen napkin, a dinner plate, bread plate, and salad plate. Next there comes a dinner fork, salad fork, dinner knife, bread knife, soup spoon, dessert spoon, a water glass, a wine glass, and a coffee cup and saucer.

The napkin should go to the left of the dinner plate, which is in the center of the setting. On the napkin may be both the salad fork and the dinner fork. Occasionally, the napkin may be displayed somewhere else in the setting or in the water glass.

To the right of the dinner plate will be the knife with the cutting edge in toward the plate and next, the spoon. To the right of the spoon will be the coffee cup and saucer. Above and to the left of the forks will be a salad plate, and just above that, a bread plate or dish. Directly above the dinner plate will be a dessert spoon, to the right of that a water glass, and then a wine glass.

The basic rule is to start from the outside and work in. The salad first, then the soup will be served, next the main course, and then dessert, and finally coffee. Remember these simple rules and learn to recognize what each utensil is for. If you do not commit any serious errors (remember the talking with the mouth full and the slurping the soup and the rude comments on someone's choice of food, and the wiping the mouth on the sleeve and a few other really objectionable acts) and stay calm, you will be fine.

Dating Etiquette

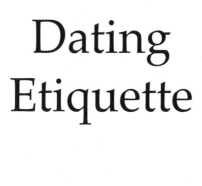

Etiquette & Dating

When the first books of etiquette were available to the public, the question of who initiated or controlled a date was not even addressed. The man initiated the date, and obeyed the rules of how far in advance to call, how to ask for a date, and how early or late to bring the young woman home. The author of that book also discussed the present era of casual dating and how some of the old rules no longer applied. The book was Emily Post's *Etiquette*, first published in 1922.

A discussion of current dating etiquette is complicated. There is the question of who asks for the date. It is still mostly a case of the man initiating the date; however, it is neither uncommon anymore for the woman to do the asking, nor is it considered inappropriate.

The next issue, and something I have already discussed, is whether the woman wishes the man to follow traditional rules such as opening doors or holding chairs, or whether this is a more open and casual relationship (even to quite formal events).

Rich Gosse in a 1995 article wrote about three issues that come up most often during dates:

- Who initiates the date?

- Who controls the date?

- Who pays?

Gosse discussed these items in some detail, yet admitted that there are no—or very few—rules for dating in America today. I discussed earlier the need to talk with a prospective date about what his or her wishes might be. From the man's point of view, the first question on initiation is not always easy to answer. The second is more difficult. And the third is a toss-up.

While recent research shows us that a large percentage of dates are still initiated by the man, it seems to be by preference rather than rule. As far as who controls the date, control may no longer even be the right description. A woman may wish to choose where the date takes place, what is appropriate as far as dress, the hours of the date, who drives, the meeting place, and so on.

As far as paying, the recent surveys show that men are still paying most of the time, but the percentage is declining. Many women prefer the traditional payment arrangement. In practical terms, a woman still only makes approximately 72 percent of what a man is paid for the same job, and may simply think the man ought to pick up the tab.

In conclusion, discuss the entire dating arrangement and do what is comfortable for you in these three areas. No matter what, a man should treat a lady like a lady. The little courtesies still apply, and they will always be appropriate.

Dating

There are a number of issues here, among them—what age to starting dating, what type of dates to participate in, and how to behave on a date. Parents and youth rarely agree on the subject of when to begin dating. Teens seem to think they are ready a long time before concerned parents are willing to see them go out the door with a perfect (or not so perfect) stranger, off to who knows where. In all truth, this is usually a matter of negotiation between the teen and the parents.

In addition, there may be a perceived difference between a "group" date and activity with a group of friends, and the traditional pairing off of boy and girl. As far as one-on-one dating (watching your little girl go out the door with a shaggy looking character in a beat-up old car) I opt for sixteen years old. The same holds true for the innocent, fresh-faced little boy leaving with that girl who looks "much older" than he does. Parents can be of great assistance by discussing this age-of-dating issue with a son or daughter long before it is a reality to avoid confrontation and misunderstanding. It is also important to have this understanding when schools, friends, and even other parents are organizing dating-type parties for youth of thirteen and fourteen years old.

The type of dating can also be important from an etiquette perspective as well as a social perspective. Young people in a group can "practice" those manners the parents have so carefully taught them in a group setting with much less pressure and become more at ease in social and public situations.

Learning manners with your friends and from your friends can also be much easier for the teen as the peer pressure can be a good influence. Going to activities with a group offers a much needed learning period for social behavior and easiness in moving into the more personal relationships that will naturally follow such leisurely conduct.

I will not discuss here behavior outside the rules of manners and etiquette—except those that may breach good taste. This publication is not the arena of this topic; however, hopefully, it is covered by parents and friends. I may refer back to a previous chapter and remind the young that good manners are always in order and even suggest some return to the Victorian ideal. It is still preferable to offer a lady your arm as you walk or as she ascends or descends a stairway, or offer your hand as she enters or exits an automobile, or steady her chair as she is seated for dinner or at a party.

It is preferable to be polite in your conversation and quiet in your manner—not to boast or be loud, and to be mindful of your language. In a more modern sense, it is important to communicate with a date and for the young man to certainly treat a young lady as an intellectual equal.

How does one request the company of a member

of the opposite gender? There are two schools of thought on this issue.

Some experts on the fine art of asking for a date suggest that nature will surely take its course. In other terms, a young man in his own bumbling way will get around to asking a young woman for a date, and that is all that is necessary. Refinement of the process will surely come with experience. I suppose if you believe in the sink-or-swim method, that is all right; however, I am somewhat concerned with the aftermath of the bumbling ways of young men (and nowadays, young women). I believe some instruction—or at least suggestion—should be made along these lines.

Informally, it would only be necessary to advise the young man to call the young woman on the telephone and politely ask the young woman to join him at a certain event. Even the informal date is not quite that simple—the question here being one of consideration. If this is just a movie, a house party with friends, or a walk along the beach, the request can be made a few days in advance. If more time is needed for preparation, more time should be given.

So, if asking to attend a dinner party, a dance, a concert, or another event requiring new clothes, shoes, or a hairdo, give the young woman more time. Never call on the day of the date unless you know this person very well or the date, or nondate, requires no preparation at all.

When asking for a date face-to-face, it is easy to make some amount of small talk, relax, and then describe the event so the young lady knows what to expect and where you are going while she considers her answer. Tell her very clearly where you are going and what you want to do. Don't ever ask, "What are you doing Friday night?" or "Do you have anything planned on Sunday?" She probably does not want to tell you if she has anything planned for Friday, nor does she wish to admit that she has nothing planned for Sunday. You may simply state, "I have tickets to the symphony on Friday and would very much like to have you join me," or "Would you please have dinner with me on Sunday evening?" Now the ball is in her court and she must decide how to respond, but you have given her sufficient information on which to make a decision.

Now what is the proper response to the request? Perhaps proper is not the right word for this generation, but something more on the lines of effective.

At this point, the average girl may not know how she wishes to respond. We really should put all the egos and the giddiness or the possible repulsion out of the picture and simply say either, "Thank you, I would love to go", or "I appreciate your asking me out, but I don't think we have much in common and would rather not go."

Now think about this ladies: you can be so much in charge at this point, but also so gracious. Whether you are facing your suitor personally or speaking on the telephone, you are warm. There is a smile in your voice and this person knows that you are sincere.

I could go into more detail of blind dates or dating someone you do not know very well, where even the most well-mannered rejection or rebuff can be met with a very negative and potentially serious reaction. However, the caution is simply to know who you are dating. Avoid getting into a situation where a person you know little about will not accept a refusal for further dating and becomes very offensive or even violent.

On a lighter note, I am talking about early dating where you are learning all this wonderful stuff about how to treat each other. The young lady in our situation is still living at home, or perhaps staying with an aunt or grandparent for the summer. The young man should always be prepared to meet the parents or the adult in the house when he comes to pick up his date.

The girl then must be prepared to make a comfortable and intelligent introduction of the date to the parents. Well-mannered parents also will greet the date warmly and see the two of them on their way to a pleasant evening. Parents should avoid putting this poor kid on the spot with thinly veiled orders or poor jokes about being home on time or "don't do anything I wouldn't" sort of warnings. The rules of the house need to be aired with the son or daughter before the arrival of the often terrified date.

Breaking a Date

The sensitive area of breaking a date as a consideration of manners deserves a bold heading. One of these areas of bad judgment is breaking a date with someone to whom we have made a commitment if we "get a better offer."

In some circles, this practice is overlooked; however, if we are truly to be considered a lady or a gentleman, it is most important that our word or commitment be valued. If it becomes absolutely necessary to break a date for reasons of health, a family emergency, or a work issue, give the person you have promised to see as much advance notice as possible and a full explanation of the legitimate reason. Breaking a date on a whim or to go with someone else is always bad manners and will leave your word and your character in question.

Taking Her Home

While I realize that dating is different now and is considered more equal, and many women do not wish any special handling, I will not discuss "taking him home." Here, I will address gentlemanly behavior, and the lady may take her cue from these guidelines.

Remember that many of the ideas of how to treat a lady from the Victorian period had to do with the safety and comfort of the lady. Not only is it in good form to escort a lady to her door, it is, in many situations, a very real issue of considering the safety of the lady.

If a lady lives on an unlighted street or in an apartment complex or an unsecured building, it is especially important to see that she is safely home. Even if the lady is in no potential danger, you can see that the root of manners is more than appearance. The man or woman who exhibits genuine concern will always have good manners.

When you arrive, do you just pull to a stop, fling the door open, and say, "Thanks, kiddo!"? Only if you want her to vanish from your life forever. Even if you do, you don't treat her like that. Offer her your arm and walk her to the door. Say your goodnight, and if she is a real lady she will hand you her key, you will unlock the door and open it, and if the room is dark you will enter the room ahead of her and turn on the light. You will then walk back into the hall and wait to be invited in. If the room is lighted, you will simply hand her the key and wait for an invitation in or a good night.

Some of the etiquette experts will discuss parking problems and traffic and say under certain conditions and in a modern society it is acceptable to stop at the curb, reach over, and let the lady out if it appears she is safe or if there is a doorman or someone to escort her to her door. However, if Sir Walter Raleigh can give up his cape to a mud puddle, you can park and walk her to the door. Remember, a gentleman is always a gentleman—he thinks enough of his behavior that it comes as second nature.

If you are always thinking of how your date, or partner, or wife should be treated, you will pay attention; the actions will be natural, far more appealing, and much more graceful.

At the Door

Unless you have dated the person you have just escorted to the door very frequently, standing at the door can be an awkward few moments. This is another time and place when small talk is quite appropriate. Just relax, discuss the movie, dinner, common friends, or something else uncomplicated.

After a few moments of this, you simply say that you enjoyed the evening. If it was a great date, you may wish to say that you would like to see this person again or would like to go out again. However, this is not mandatory.

Informal Entertaining Etiquette

Informal Entertaining

Informal entertaining includes buffet dinners, barbecues, luncheons, cocktail parties, picnics, informal dances, and house parties. Although classified as informal, there are still rules, and acceptable behavior is still important in any setting.

Dishing & Serving

When serving guests, servers move around the table counter-clockwise, serving from the left of a person. Serving may begin with the female guest of honor, but never with the host or hostess who are always served last.

A sideboard is usually where the food available for seconds is kept. If you are at a buffet or barbecue, do not go back to the serving line until everyone else has had a chance to get their first serving. Quite generally if you notice the host eating, then you may assume that all have been served and go in for seconds.

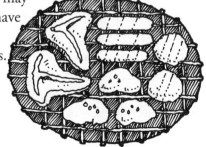

Host & Hostess Duties

It is the duty of the host or hostess to mingle with guests, to introduce guests to each other, and to see that each person is occupied in an entertaining manner. It is his or her job to see that the party flows—that there are no awkward lapses in which people stand around with nothing to do.

It is his or her job to see that the food is on time and hot or cold as the case may be; that guests are informed of what is expected of them—this can be as subtle as leading them into a room where there are drinks and music. The hosts should provide a smoking area and notify guests of its presence.

It is also his or her job to monitor drinking of alcohol, to ensure that no one leaves intoxicated unless attended by a designated driver. It is further his or her job to end the party, by sending off the last of the guests with a smile and a warm farewell.

Guest Duties

It is the guests' duty to arrive within 15 to 20 minutes of the appointed time, or to call with a plausible excuse as to the delay. It is also their duty to watch for hints when it is time to depart and to not dwell until the wee hours while the host and hostess are yawning.

It is the guests' responsibility to become full with what the hostess has served for dinner. If seconds are not offered, it is best to not ask unless you know there is sufficient extra.

All guests should mingle among themselves and assist the hostess by engaging the wallflowers.

Guests should refrain from consuming an excess of alcohol and should not make an issue of it if the hosts choose not serve alcohol. Ask where to smoke before lighting up a cigar, cigarette, or pipe.

The guest should always seek out the host and/or hostess to issue a thank you prior to departure.

Mingling & Dancing

To mingle is to visit with numerous people throughout the evening, rather than devoting all of your time and attention on one or two persons. Granted it is more important for the host and hostess to mingle than for a guest, but it is a good habit to help them out when possible by seeking out the wallflowers and offering some of your time to draw them out. It does not take long, 15 to 20 minutes is more than sufficient time with someone who's company you don't really enjoy.

Gentlemen should always dance once with the hostess, the guest of honor (if it's a she), the ladies seated on either side of him, and the first and last dance of the evening with his wife or partner. He should also never leave a lady to escort herself off of the dance floor.

Ladies may accept or politely decline to dance with any person who requests without worry of insulting the issuer of the invitation. The only time she may not refuse is on the floor when a gentleman "cuts-in," nor should her current partner refuse. Ladies should not dance more than a time or two with any man other than her date.

House Parties & Overnight Guests

This may be classified as the most "informal" type of entertainment, especially if you are entertaining people who just happen to drop in on you. The true test of a good host is presence under fire. A planned party with invitations and planned activities for a night's stay is different from the harried situation of unplanned guests.

A good house party need not entail stuffing as many people as you can into your house. Know how many you can accommodate while still leaving yourself time to enjoy the guests and the occasion. If you are an energetic host or hostess and large groups do not bother you, go for it.

Think about the party, the occasion, the activities, and the personalities you are bringing together, then plan accordingly.

House Party Invitations

For an informal house party, the invitations are often phoned; however, if some of the guests are out of town, the invitation is written on notepaper. A note on personalized stationery is preferred.

In the note, be specific as to whom you wish to attend. This is helpful to your guests if they have children. Specify if the children are invited. If this is to be an overnight event, you should give information about the activities planned so guests may plan clothing, etc.

Whether your invitation is the informal phone call or the mailed note, you need to address transportation details. If there is public transport or your guests are arriving by airplane, give them flight schedules or train times and arrange to pick them up on arrival.

March 15th

Dear Jane;

Bob and I are hoping that Edward, the children, and you can spend Easter weekend with us at the farm in Newbury. If you leave just after lunch on April 14, you can easily be here for dinner at 5:00. Then, the children can play outside until it is dark. If you catch the 214 just off Lands End Rd., you can be here in plenty of time. The spring flowers are beautiful now and there is a small lake nearby where we can take the children fishing. We do so hope you can join us.

Affectionately,
Barbara

Informal Invitations

There is an informal type of invitation. This can include the telephone or e-mail. If you are well acquainted with someone, it is acceptable to send an informal note inviting them to a casual event.

Informal invitations can be extended over the telephone and sometimes are preferable, as they give a personal touch and allow for some individuality to special guests, such as grandparents and other family members.

When sending a note you may use a card with your name on it, including the address. You can also use a printed invitation, many of which are printed for just the occasion you need and are quite clever and convenient. As far as e-mail, you can add graphics and even some sound if you wish, further personalizing the message.

Guest Rooms

If we all had the accommodations we would wish for our friends and guests, we would simply call the maid to make certain the guest room or rooms were in order for the evening. Since most of us do not live in mansions with plenty of guest rooms we must make do, and our friends will understand. Your hospitality can be just as sincere and just as appreciated by your friends, but there are a few simple rules.

Some have a den with a sofa that will make into a nice bed; others have some accommodation in a family room or a bedroom currently not in use. Most of us, however, will have to make some temporary adjustment and move a family member out of a room. Children can be gathered together in a den or family room with sleeping bags or cots and be perfectly happy.

In the summer, outdoor sleeping is a big evening

for them. Be certain the children are in agreement with the arrangements and are not grumbling to the guests about being displaced.

If you are rearranging junior's room for some of your guests, be certain to put on clean linens. Have fresh towels handy, and clean out at least part of the closet for guests' clothes.

If junior has a bed that looks like a race car or a jungle animal, you may want to camouflage it with a quilt. Also, move toys and trendy posters out of the room. I assume your guest knows you and your family well enough to understand and possess at least a minimal sense of humor.

If you are fortunate enough to have a guest room, there are a few things to remember. It is true that every host or hostess should spend a night or two in their own guest room to test its comfort level. If this is not convenient, there are a few things to check. Make certain the bed is not a backbreaker. Check the linens to see that they are fresh.

If there is a guest bath, be certain the faucets work and do not drip all night. Further, see that there is fresh soap in the sink dish as well as the tub or shower, an outlet for an electric razor, a place to keep a toothbrush, a mirror, and decent lighting.

Take a few tips from your favorite hotel and put some of the little extras in the bath that you enjoy. You should also provide facial tissues and tooth-paste. You can purchase small bottles of shampoo or bath salts, and make certain the towels are large enough and clean and dry.

You may also want to include a robe or slippers, magazines or reading material, a portable TV or radio, ashtrays if they smoke (or no ashtrays if you wish they wouldn't), and even a morning or even-ing snack.

What you wish to do depends on how well you know your guests. If these people have not stayed with you before, every little thing you do can make a big difference in how comfortable they feel.

The real purpose of the guest room is not just a place to sleep, but a room away from all the rush of a house suddenly busy and overcrowded. Even if it is just a few minutes before bedtime, be certain your guests have a place away from everyone else where they can relax.

Picnic Planning

In most parts of the country, from April until September, the weather is usually cooperative enough to allow for the great international event called the "picnic." The picnic can be an informal meal on the grass somewhere or a traveling culinary extravaganza, with china and silver and all the amenities.

The picnic can be something that you decide you want to throw for some of your friends or you can turn it into a potluck surprise event. If you wish to be the complete host, you may prepare a menu, call your friends and invite them, and tell them where and what time.

For a fun type of party, plan what you and your friends or family would like, make the assignments or suggestions, and put an entire day together including activities, games, or sports.

The point is, whether it is a formal dinner or a

picnic, be gracious and detailed in the invitation and the expectations for the event. If the picnic is to be at the beach, suggest blankets and deck chairs or beach towels and let people know times and directions if necessary. If you are going to the mountains and will be late into the evening, be certain to remind your guests to bring a jacket or a sweater and perhaps a blanket.

Also, make arrangements for children. Let parents know what type of games or activities you have planned; and if you want someone to bring a particular dish for the meal, let him or her know.

Sometimes, with all the excitement of a picnic, it is difficult to get children to eat. If you simply let each family plan the meal for their children, it is likely they will know what the children like to eat and the day can be more successful.

Picnics really should be fun and festive. You can plan all kinds of colorful and decorative meals and pack them in a basket or cooler, then spread out a real feast in the woods or at a park. While these meals are meant to be casual, you need not throw manners to the wind. You can still lay a very nice table even if it is on the ground or on a cement table in a public park.

One of the truly enjoyable and practical party ideas is to share favorite dishes with friends and sample many kinds of food. This is especially fun with different ethnic foods and traditional dishes of other countries.

Hosting a Picnic

It is a brave and sturdy soul who decides to plan a picnic, chooses the menu, and invites the guests. However, if you like this sort of thing, keep in mind that you are there to enjoy yourself.

Remember, it may be an entirely different group of friends or acquaintances you invite to a picnic than to a cocktail party. A supper on the patio is quite civilized and charming and as close to an outdoors adventure as some guests may want.

A picnic is not for the faint of heart. Keep this in mind when putting together the guest list. Select friends or family who you know will enjoy the outing and the culinary fare, and who are not inconvenienced by the great outdoors.

If you know that Ursula and her new friend Robert are both "hothouse plants" and will wither in the potential dust and mosquito environment of the "pasture party," leave them off the guest list;

you will be doing everyone a favor. Nothing ruins a fun and informal outdoor party like one or two people who continually whine about the heat or the bugs or the food being cold or a little bit of sand.

Find a group of low-maintenance companions who will look forward to walking in the woods, running in the surf, a good game of softball, and having a great dinner or lunch on a blanket.

Now that you have the right group together and have planned a great day, you must still be a good host. This also means planning some convenience and a good meal for your guests.

Select your location with comfort in mind. If you are going to the beach, choose a place that is easily accessible (knowing it may also be more crowded), where you can drive close to the picnic site or have some type of conveyance for all of the gear and food. If you have this great little secret hideaway, your guests might not want to slog a mile through the sand to get there with a banquet on their backs. The same goes for some mountain locations; don't have everyone completely exhausted from the hike before the picnic even begins.

In addition, take some precautions to minimize the discomforts that can be predicted. Plan to take some sort of shade with you if hot and sunny, or shelter for a surprise thunderstorm.

Know that you will be able to prepare a good meal that is fully cooked when you are ready to eat. What your guests do not want to hear is "I sure hope this works," as you begin to prepare the meal.

Decide if you want a hot meal or all cold, ready-to-eat kinds of foods. Carrying propane or other fuels or firewood can be very tedious. Also, be aware of local rules and regulations about fires and cooking in outdoor locations. Usually, the best advice is to keep it quite simple. You may wish to cook a meat dish over a fire or on a small and easily carried hibachi or other cooker, and then serve cold dishes on the side.

If you are making and packing sandwiches in advance, be careful with tomatoes, mayonnaise, and other soft or runny ingredients that can make a good sandwich a soggy mess before you arrive at the appointed place. You can make a wonderful and portable meal with cold chicken (roasted or fried), cold meats with salads, sliced or cubed melons, rolls or biscuits that do not crush like sliced bread, and the most portable of desserts: cookies.

Be certain you have plenty of cold drinks, and you can add other fresh fruits. There are containers and wrappings now that will allow you to take along frosted cakes and fancy desserts if you really want a gourmet picnic; however, ease and convenience are usually the rule on a picnic.

Pack It In, Pack It Out

Good outdoor manners are important. As usual, manners have a very practical basis. In the outdoors, whether the beach, the mountains, or the local park, cleaning up is important.

Just like the dinner party in a nice home, when the meal is over, you must leave everything just as you found it—sometimes better. This brings us back to the matter of how you carry items into your picnic site. Plastics are wonderful for their utility and convenience; however, they do not dissolve or decay and they don't go away. Be certain you bring plenty of trash bags, cloths for wiping off tables and soap for washing up if you wish to clean the dishes before you leave.

I recall many years ago visiting one of the beautiful Hawaiian islands and walking along a very famous beach with the warm Pacific waters lapping at the shore and the blue sky overhead. My wife and I took a little hike inland from the beach and were appalled at the mountains of trash hidden in the trees and brush. Fortunately, the state of Hawaii became aware of this mess and things are cleaned up (at great expense). It is one of the simplest but most important manners you can learn: "pack it in, pack it out." Don't mess up nature; it is everybody's house.

Barbecue Time

The barbecue is a lot like a picnic but closer to the conveniences of the kitchen, so you can be a little more orderly and formal.

At a barbecue, you can lay out a colorful, proper table and still get the feel of the outdoors. You can use your own dishes (not the china), or you can use some of the very colorful plastic or paper products that are now available. You can even set a specific theme; there are western parties, beach parties, clambakes, or whatever.

With folding tables and portable lighting of all varieties, folding or lightweight outdoor furniture, bright umbrellas, and any number of cooking options, you are ready to go and only a few feet away.

Setting the table gives you many options. You will need a table near where you are cooking to hold the food plus the utensils, etc.

For eating you may have a number of tables or a

buffet table, and chairs for the guests to sit in while they eat. Folding tables or wooden picnic tables are readily available from rental businesses specializing in parties.

Long tables can be covered with brightly colored checked or floral-print cloths; centerpieces can be made of flowers, driftwood, cowboy boots, sand pails, or whatever peaks your imagination. The barbecue can be as formal as you wish. The popular choice is convenience. That means going with the paper or plastic plates and cups (flatware is optional), paper napkins, or anything else that can be discarded after the meal, so you are not up all night washing dishes after everyone leaves.

The host or hostess is normally the cook at these events, but that is not a hard-and-fast rule. Sometimes, other members of the family or one of the well-acquainted guests may try a hand at the fire. Cooking at a barbecue, however, is a social activity and one most people wish to keep for themselves.

Now, if you are a poor cook, even with hamburgers and hotdogs, you may still be the social butterfly and the toast of the evening, but let someone else do the cooking so the guests will come back another time.

If the host is at all adequate and can at least be monitored through the grilling of meat, the a cohost is well placed to run the evening and get all the other food items on the table in an orderly manner.

Even a buffet requires some organization and management. At barbecue meals, as at picnics, it is often well and very hospitable to ask guests to bring a special dish or drink or dessert to share.

At a barbecue or picnic, games and activities can round out the day and keep the children occupied while the meal is being prepared. You may have the kind of yard or lawn that can accommodate a game of croquet or horseshoes. Some may want to play catch, run races, play an organized game of tag with the children, or go for a swim.

Depending upon your budget and your guests, you may also want to consider some type of music. Music is a wonderful addition to any gathering. You can have subtle background music or you may hire a polka band and offer a dance party.

Outdoor evenings lend themselves to guitars, a piano on the patio, or even a mariachi band, if it fits the mood of the party.

Before you schedule the music, of course, you must also consider the setting and the neighbors if there are any nearby. The music does not have to be live, especially if there is a budget question. If you know your guests and most of you share the same musical tastes, you may wish to just put on some of your favorite CDs or tapes. If you want to make this a music party, have everyone bring a few selections and listen and discuss them.

Alfresco

Alfresco, or eating outdoors, is a popular way to entertain. Many who cannot accommodate a large group indoors use the backyard as a roomy place to spread the feast and guests. There are a few simple rules to follow when dining outside.

As the guest: Don't skip ahead of the line just because someone allows you to "cut-in" front. Make certain to pick up and dispose of your own paperware. Locate your host and hostess and thank them before leaving.

Avoid feeding any pets roaming about (although there shouldn't be any.) If children are present, be very careful to monitor your liquor. Avoid picking your teeth in the presence of others.

If seating is upon the ground or in a chair without a table, avoid resting your plate directly on your lap. However, if the plate is flimsy, you may rest it on your napkin on your lap.

Adhere to the rules of finger food—if it drips, has sauce on it, or is limp, use a fork.

Don't assume that, just because you are outside, smoking anywhere is permissible. Inquire where the smoking section is before lighting up.

As the host or hostess: supply—plenty of napkins, complete silver or plasticware settings. It is helpful to supply sturdy paper plates with wicker or plastic paper plate holders. Place salt and pepper sets on each serving table. Have a trash receptacle for every ten persons located conveniently around the area.

Designate a smoking table away from the rest of the crowd. Place two large, sand-filled coffee cans labeled ashtray on either end of that table. This takes the guesswork out of it for the smokers and nonsmokers alike.

Provide specific seating for seniors, if this is a "blanket" picnic.

Potlucks

It seems almost silly to have a section on manners at potlucks. Technically most of the rules or suggestions from dining alfresco would apply here. The main difference is that you take a dish to the affair, rather than having someone else serve you a complete meal.

I will only offer a few (albeit crucial) ideas concerning the potluck that differ from the section on dining alfresco.

If you are taking a hot dish, pack it so that it stays hot and the reverse for cold dishes. This is more than good etiquette—this is a safety issue. Food should not be left to reach that crucial temperature where food poisoning becomes an issue.

Take a serving utensil for each dish you bring. If the dish requires something special (soup needs bowls for example) bring along some throw away dishes just in case.

If you are contributing a dish from an old family secret recipe that you don't want to share, be up front and polite about it when someone asks.

When dishing your plate, try and sample a daub of everything so that no one's feelings are hurt that their dish went untouched. I have seen this happen and it makes me feel sorry for the dish's creator.

If the potluck is held someplace where a main dish (large pot of chili, etc.) is cooked, and clean up will be done, offer to help with the clean up. Potlucks really are a group effort in all phases of the meal, including the cleaning up.

Open House or Housewarming

The open house or housewarming is just that; your house is open to all guests during the times you have specified in your invitation. The invitation, again, may be a personal phone call, a note in the mail, or an e-mail. You should specify the hours, address, and attire (if this is important). If you prefer that guests do not bring gifts, please make it known in the invitation.

You may plan the food in different ways at an open house. You may wish to spread a buffet, or just have some finger food, chips and dip, or nuts and drinks.

If it is to be a buffet, then there are buffet rules to deal with—keeping the food fresh, and so on.

If this is a holiday open house, you will want to have holiday music, decorations, and food; and that becomes a bit more detailed and complex.

If it is an open house for a wedding anniversary

or for someone who has been away for a time, you may wish to have a special cake, some type of welcome for those attending, and more in the way of refreshments.

If this is a housewarming for a new home, a remodeled house, or a vacation residence, a gift for the house or its occupants is in order.

When you have an open house or house-warming, there is always the question of where to put the children and how much of the house to open up or share with your guests. During some seasons of the year, such as Christmas or summer-time, some neighborhoods hold open house tours to view decorations, Christmas lights, or gardens.

If yours is the home featured in the open house or tour, you may wish to make signs or directions to areas open to the visitors and areas that are private to the family.

Unless the children are very young and already put to bed, they should assist in welcoming the guests, serving food, or giving directions. This is a great way to improve their own manners and for them to learn social skills. If the little ones are in bed, that area is off limits.

If you are one of the friends, a neighbor, or just a curious guest at an open house, there are more rules.

- When entering, wipe feet or remove shoes.

- Be courteous and thank the host and hostess for allowing you to visit.

- Do not poke around in closets or cupboards.

- Do not open doors that are purposely closed.

- Do not ask the cost of knickknacks, paintings, or furniture.

- Be careful of what you pick up or touch. If you simply cannot resist lifting some treasure from its resting place, ask permission of the host and graciously accept his answer.

- Do not leave glasses on good pieces of furniture to make rings.

- Do not leave bits of food lying around.

- Do not voice a negative opinion of the décor or furnishings.

The hours for party giving and entertaining are important. Dinner in the United States varies from one section of the country to another, but is generally from 6:00 to 8:00 in the evening. Sunday meals vary even more. Often the main meal or the family dinner is at midday rather than in the evening. This has come from a long tradition in Middle America of eating the daily meal at noon as a break in farming activity and the Sunday meal right after church services.

In some foreign countries, they may eat lunch from noon until 2:00 in the afternoon and dinner at 9:00 or 10:00 in the evening. Often the best rule is to be aware of the custom of your area.

If your guests are accustomed to eating at 6:00 each evening, making them wait until ten is very discourteous, and for some, quite uncomfortable. Additionally, if you announce dinner is to be at 8:00 p.m., begin serving dinner right at 8:00 p.m. Times are almost sacred in some communities. Find out from neighbors and friends when the customary times are for a brunch, a dinner, a wedding breakfast, or a wedding, and try to schedule yours so the guests are most comfortable.

Shower Time

A shower may be given for a number of purposes. The most common are baby showers and wedding showers. I will discuss wedding showers later when we look into the whole social order of weddings.

A shower may also be given for older children, for a newly arriving clergyperson, or a housewarming for a new neighbor.

The setting for a shower may be a brunch-type social, a luncheon, an afternoon tea, or a dinner. The common denominator of the shower is the giving of gifts. A shower may suggest a specific type of gift; many bridal showers now are specific to rooms of the house or days of the week.

The invitation to a shower should be written, or at least sent in the mail. The difference here is a specially prepared or engraved invitation or one you can buy in a card or stationery shop that is preprinted for the type of shower you are giving. Unless you have money to throw around, the colorful type from the card shop works fine. You may add details to these, such as time and address, the gender of the baby, or color scheme suggestions. You may want to give some idea of the type of refreshments, also. The more information you can give your guests, the better.

Generally, a baby shower is given in the evening, as is a shower for a new neighbor or clergyperson.

Baby showers are usually only attended by female friends and family. The conventional baby shower is given prior to the birth of the baby, but this is changing. A thoughtful friend may organize a shower for a friend when the baby is few months old and early infant clothes have been outgrown.

A shower may also be a surprise party. In this case, the guests may bring the refreshments or a light meal. In the case of a surprise shower for a new mom, give her a little notice before the guests begin to arrive so she can make herself and the baby more party worthy.

The gifts and the presentations of the gifts are also important. The gifts for a new neighbor or a new baby need to be displayed and shared by everyone. The big difference between a shower and other celebrations is that it is much like a birthday party, where everyone views the gifts as opened and talks and laughs about them.

The guest of honor is set up (quite literally) in the middle of the room or some other conspicuous place and the gifts are passed, identified by giver, and opened with a great deal of excitement by all.

When the gifts are all open and the proper appreciation has been extended, it is time for the refreshments. While the eating and the conversation continues, all the gifts can then be displayed on a table or on the floor for all to admire.

Foods: Comfortable & Awkward

Some of the most terrifying moments at a dinner or party come when the food is served. If you are the host, you may want to consider the physical act of getting the morsel from plate to mouth before adding it to the list. I am not certain why we select stuffed celery, artichokes, anything on the half-shell, or pasta, because of the awkwardness of these foods.

You could make an entire meal of these dexterity- and mind-challenging items, and then distribute little disposable cameras and make it the evening's entertainment. If you do, however, attend a party or dinner where the host has dropped the gauntlet of graceful dining, here are some tips.

- Asparagus—that is small and slender should not be covered with sauce so one may pick it up and eat it with the fingers.

- Bacon—that is not crisp and has a ridge of soft fat, should be eaten with a knife and fork.

- Fresh apples and pears—may be cut into sections with core removed, then eaten with fingers.

- Oranges and bananas—may be peeled and cut into sections, then eaten with fingers.

- Salad—should not be cut up. You simply take your chances and try to get small bites.

- Fresh strawberries—may be served in a bowl with cream and then eaten with a spoon. These may also be served whole and dipped in sugar, powdered sugar, chocolate, or a fruit dip and eaten with fingers.

- Raspberries or blueberries—should be served in a bowl and eaten with a spoon.

- Fresh cherries and plums—may be eaten with the fingers. When eating fresh fruits with pits, drop the pit from your mouth into the palm of your hand, then dispose of it.

- Stewed prunes and bottled berries—are served in a bowl and eaten with a spoon. When eating cooked fruits with a pit or stone, drop the pit from your mouth into your spoon, then deposit it on the side of the plate.

- Melons—come in a variety of shapes, sizes, and degrees of eating difficulty. Some contend that one may take a slice of watermelon in both hands and eat from the rind. Unless you are at the side of the pond or dressed in a swimsuit, it should be cut into a more convenient size and eaten with a fork. Watermelons may also be cut into cubes or balls and served over sherbet, sorbet, or with a sprig of mint. Cantaloupe, casaba, honeydew, and some of the lighter and rounder melons are cut into crescent slices, then eaten with a fork, spoon, or knife.

- Cheeses, olives, small onions, and french fries—may all be eaten with the fingers.

- Lamb or pork chops—should be cut and eaten with a knife and fork as far as the major part of the center cut is concerned; then it is permissible to pick up the remaining bone and clean it off with your teeth.

- Lobster—necessitates securely grasping with the hands. The claws can be cracked and held up to the mouth. The tail can be cracked and the meat extracted with a lobster fork.

- Corn on the cob—though awkward and messy, can be eaten with the fingers. Avoid being noisy and aggressive, no matter how good it may taste.

- Chicken, game hen, or small fowl—at a formal dinner should not be eaten with the fingers. Do the best you can with a wing, using a knife and fork. If you are at home or in a less formal setting, you may pick up the wing or drumstick; however, the breast should be cut and eaten with a knife and fork.

- Grapes—are served at informal and formal dinners. When the fruit is served or passed along, do not pick off the individual grape and eat it. Break off a small bunch and put it on your plate, then pick from that smaller serving.

- Celery and pickles—may be eaten with the fingers. However, pickles covered with sauce or juices may do better with a small fork.

- Shellfish—if served on the half-shell, can be held up to the mouth, then eaten with a small fork. Using a fork, dip clams and oysters into sauce and eat all in one bite. Fried clams may be eaten with the fingers. Large fried shrimp are held in the fingers by the tail, then eaten one bite at a time. The tail is then deposited on the side of the plate.

Formal Entertaining Etiquette

Formal Entertaining

There will be a certain amount of repetition in this section, but then we learn from that which is repeated. Most of what passes for formal entertaining today is really a mixture of the formal and informal. A true formal dinner at the home of the host would require space, furnishings, china and crystal, and a staff that few people possess today.

The great dinners of European royalty are now only with the remnants of royalty and a diminishing number of wealthy families around the world.

For a legitimately formal dinner, one must be able to seat all the guests at one table; they should number at least three dozen, and you would need one footman or trained servant for every four to five people. All the silver, china, and crystal should match, and each course should be served exactly on time and must not be allowed to get chilled or tepid while waiting, depending on the dish.

Today's very formal setting is reserved for official dinners rather than in private homes. The private dinner party, however, can be a masterpiece for the host if it is done correctly. The formal dinner is probably a little less formal these days. The comfort of the guests is increased, and that is a real improvement. Some parts of the dinner or dinner party remain the same: the table setting must be completely proper (and hopefully you reach for stunning or magnificent), the guest list and handling of the invitations must be flawless, the preparation and serving of the meal must go off without a hitch, and you must be the most gracious host in the civilized world.

If you must select one of those areas in which to excel, and allow some of the others to be less than perfect, concentrate on the last one. If you are the epitome of grace, poise, and politeness, you can get by with a few flaws. Also, if we are weighing perfection of presentation and the comfort of your guests, by all means let your guests feel at home and relaxed. You will all have a more enjoyable evening.

The perfect table should be able to seat sixteen persons on each side, plus one at the head and one at the foot. Incidentally, if there are too many at the dinner and you must break them into smaller tables, it is no longer a formal dinner.

In addition, it is not possible to give a formal dinner without servants. If the guests must serve themselves either family-style at the table or from a buffet, this is not a formal dinner.

What I am discussing now is the beautiful, formal-looking dinner or dinner party that is really informal. The very formal authorities on the dining experience will suggest that the formal dinner is still possible and that you can hire footmen, butlers, waiters or waitresses, and cooks. This is quite true if you live where such people are available and are actually as good as the rate they request. In a very formal situation, if the host is not cooking and does not keep a cook on staff, he may wish to retain an excellent cook.

The cook should arrive early in the day and be thoroughly briefed on the whereabouts of all he or she will need from utensils to the food for preparation. The host will have prepared the menu in complete detail and will give the cook a precise timetable.

If you are to serve a formal dinner, you should have available all that an excellent cook or chef would need to prepare what you have instructed. It will be necessary to communicate with your new cook well in advance of the event to be certain everything will be in order and in its place when he or she arrives.

The cook also stays until all the food is prepared, served, and the cooking materials and utensils are cleaned and returned to their proper places.

The butler and footmen may be other additions to a dinner. The butler stands near or behind the host as the guests arrive and announces each guest. If the guests are not to be announced, the butler assists the host as he pleases or serves cocktails to the guests as they arrive.

In very formal circles, the butler has prepared the cocktails well in advance and is prepared for the guests as they arrive. The butler, whether temporary or house staff, should be schooled and skilled enough that he takes all the detailed niceties of seeing the new arrivals into the house off the shoulders of the host.

After the butler has seen the guests into the house, the footman will tend to their wraps and usher them into the dining room or wherever they are to be seated. As we saw before in the time of good Queen Victoria, there were enough footmen that every two persons were watched over closely. In some cases, a single footman does the duty. This is mostly to prove to your friends that you know how to do these things. One footman would be worn to a frazzle if he were to attend the guests as they were in the court of Queen Victoria.

In the modern expression of manners and the less formal way of entertaining, while still calling it "formal," you could probably dispense with the butler and the footman. But a good cook and a competent waiter or waitress or two can add a lot to the dinner and take a huge load off the host.

Selecting & Seating Guests

What must be considered in the guest list is the ability of the guests to relate to one another, and therefore have a comfortable evening. In some situations, such as formal government or business dinners, the guest list is already set. In these cases, it is important how the guests are seated to arrive at a congenial evening and avoid obvious trouble.

When seating guests, there may or may not be a guest of honor. The guest of honor need not be recognized for anything specific. Generally, the guest of honor is the eldest lady present. It can also be, at the choice of the host, someone else he has elected to honor.

The host will always seat the guest of honor on his right. The person of honor, therefore, is the person seated to the right of the host. The host enters the room first with the female guest of honor on his arm. The other guests, teamed together, follow him, with the hostess and male guest of honor entering last. The female guest of honor is seated first and the host and hostess remain standing behind their own chairs.

If there are place cards, the guests look for their proper places and the ladies are seated. The gentlemen remain standing until all the ladies are seated.

If place cards are not used, the host, from his position, directs the seating. The host will generally not seat husbands and wives together, but will seat men and women together if they are not well acquainted with their escort. Men and women who have been married for a year or less or persons who are recently engaged may be seated together.

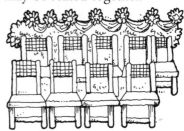

Formal Invitations

In some circles, the very formal invitation still exists and the rules and protocols are still in force. Some experts on the rules of etiquette suggest that only a written and mailed invitation is acceptable for a formal dinner. Others suggest that a telephoned invitation, and perhaps even a quick e-mail is appropriate. The point is that a very nice dinner to which you would like to invite people whom you respect and whose company you enjoy deserves an equally nice invitation.

The invitation may be engraved, printed, or handwritten. The very formal engraved invitation is written in the third person with the name of the person who is invited being handwritten. Most important with regard to the invitation is the expedience with which one need reply. This is a practical rule of etiquette.

When you reply to the invitation to a formal

dinner, just as the barbecue or picnic, it affords the host information on how many guests to expect. This helps in all areas from planning the menu to the seating arrangements. To wait until the last minute is simply bad taste, and shows little consideration for the host.

You should reply just as invited, whether as Mr. and Mrs., or John and Mary, and repeat the date and time so there will be no question as to how you understood the invitation.

If a couple gets an invitation and only one of them can attend, the acceptance is written first so the host may see who is coming, followed by the regret that the other individual cannot attend.

If you cannot attend or do not wish to attend, then graciously decline. The note of regret, should be again, sent in the same formal manner in which the invitation was received. In the note of regret, state very briefly the reason you cannot attend (illness, out of town, etc.). Even if you are not planning to attend and must send a note of regret, send this as punctually as you would a note of acceptance; because you are not going is no reason to be tardy on your reply. Never play the odds and accept and then not show up. A no-show is the worst of bad manners.

When specifically requesting a reply, the person sending the invitation will almost always include the letters R.S.V.P. on the invitation. Occasionally the invitation will specify "R.S.V.P. regrets," which means they will expect you unless you write or call and say you cannot attend. R.S.V.P. comes from the French phrase "Répondez s'il vouz plaît," or Please Reply. This is often omitted on informal invitations, with the host assuming you will attend if you can. Even in an informal situation, it is best to reply and let the host know whether you are coming or not, and thank him for the invitation.

Formal Invitation Styles

The very formal invitation is always engraved—never printed. This hard rule is bending a bit these days, and in most cases, a nice printed invitation will suffice. I suppose in some circles, the judgment of one's social status begins with the quality of one's invitation, the name of the engraver, the rag content of the paper, and so on. If we are to convince the majority of people that good manners are practical and a matter of good will and courtesy, we need to do away with those arrogant ideas.

There is some practicality in what is called a "fill-in" invitation. In this form, the main information on the invitation, such as the name of the host and hostess and the address, are engraved. The details such as to whom the invitation is addressed, the specific occasion, date, and time are handwritten on the invitation in black ink. The type of social event can also be written in, such as black tie, white tie, etc. Invitations are written, in the third person:

Mr. and Mrs. John Jones
Request the pleasure of your company
at dinner
on Saturday, May the twelfth
at eight o'clock
41 East Edgewood Drive
Atlanta, GA 79702

R.S.V.P.

When two friends are sending the invitations together, the form is the same but both names are used, such as: Miss Ann Walters and Miss Jo Hess.

The formal invitation can also be handwritten in total on a personal formal writing paper, preferably white. Most persons who have acquired personal stationery or who send a lot of invitations have the address printed or engraved on the writing paper. If this is not the case, simply write the address in as part of the invitation.

If your handwriting is poor or impossible to read, have someone who has good penmanship address the invitations for you. If you have plenty of time and talent, calligraphy is a nice touch.

On a formal invitation, a telephone number is never included. Now, there is another school of thought about formal invitations. I have said the address may be written if it is not a part of the note or invitation card. Formal persons insist that an address is not part of the engraved invitation card.

For the most formal occasions, the invitation may include a monogram in color or embossed in white, or a coat of arms—but never an address. One may choose how formal to be. There are invitations for every occasion, but the basic rules apply.

If you wish to see examples of everything from a country club cocktail party to a formal public gathering, I would refer you to the public library.

In this new age, it is permissible to send a formal invitation by telephone. E-mail still seems a little casual for a formal occasion. There is an appropriate form for telephone invitations. The phone call may be taken by the intended guest, but is usually given by an employee or butler.

The person speaking on behalf of the host says, "Will you please say that Mr. Samuel Adams invites Mr. and Mrs. Smith to dine on Saturday night the fifteenth at 7:30 p.m., formal, Mr. Adams's number is monument four one hundred." The person taking the message writes it down and then repeats it back so there are no mistakes. This can be followed up with a reminder card—also engraved.

The telephoned acceptance takes the same form: "Will you please tell Mr. Adams that Mr. and Mrs. Washington will be happy to accept his invitation to dine on Saturday night the fifteenth at 7:30 p.m." or regret, etc.

Meals & Food

For the host of overnight guests, breakfast is important, especially if no prior plans were made about tastes and habits. If you, as the guest, are a late sleeper, look on this stay as a vacation, have legitimate health problems dealing with diet, or do not need much for breakfast, tell the host in advance. If you are just a picky eater, put your manners in front of your attitude and graciously eat what you are served. If you have a distaste for something, you may politely skip the item; however, if you put it on your plate, then you are committed.

The host should inform guests the evening before of breakfast arrangements, giving guests time to communicate to the host specific needs. However, if the only choice is ham and eggs, at 6:00 a.m., smile and go to breakfast on time.

Petiquette

Pets

There are some rules and should be some consideration, and common sense used when dealing with the pets of neighbors and friends and when expecting others to deal with your pets.

Large or unruly pets should be controlled and out of the way when company comes. When visiting, if pets are a part of the household and are not bothersome, deal with them. I have a friend who trains and grooms dogs and expensive show horses. He appears to be the kind of person who would be at ease with any type of furry creature. However, I found out the hard way that he was absolutely terrified of cats.

When you have guests over, try to discern or even ask how they feel about animals. If you are not certain, keep animals under control or out of sight. It is usually not the responsibility of the animal to make an adjustment to the situation. Either the visitor or the pet's owner must take control.

As the guest, never assume you know the animal. For instance, many humans think that a dog who is wagging his tail is friendly. This is not always true and many times these people get bitten. Additionally, people tend to think smaller dogs are safer than larger dogs, or more easily cared for or trained; however, this is not necessarily true.

People also think that it is okay to approach a dog or a cat and pet them, it is not. Many people are bitten by animals each year because they take the liberty of petting an animal they meet. We tend to overstep our bounds with animals when we would not think of doing so with another human.

Pet owners should take the time to give their animal quality attention, teaching it manners from an early age, and getting help from a professional. Often, if you are already having problems, new and appropriate behavior can be reached in eight to twelve weeks of minimal but consistent work.

One universal problem with pets is the care and disposal of animal waste. Dogs, or rather their owners, are the worst offenders. There are many more dog ordinances now than in the past; however, the owner must take care of the animal—the animal does not know the law. Here are some basic rules of canine etiquette.

- When walking a dog, keep it on a leash unless you are in one of a growing number of parks or areas designated for dogs to run free.

- Never allow your dog to run free in the neighborhood at night.

- If your dog accidentally messes up the sidewalk or someone's yard, clean it up. When you go for a walk with your pet, be prepared to clean up after him.

- If your dog is a chronic barker, find a way to cure this problem or bring the dog in the house.

- If you have a dog (or cat) that sheds hair, cover the chairs and couches or clean them before company arrives.

- Do not allow a dog to jump on guests. Many people are afraid by this behavior even from a friendly mutt. It can also be very embarrassing.

- Do not take a dog to visit friends or relatives without them knowing that your best friend is going to accompany you. This situation is made worse if you are staying over and they have made no accommodation for the animal.

- Never assume everyone treats a dog the same way you do. It is not a good idea to feed a dog from the table or feed them table scraps. Do not feed a friend's dog from the table while you are a guest. If your dog is present at meals with guests, make it clear whether it is allowed to feed your dog from the table.

Today people give liberties to pets that children only wish they enjoyed. In many places, there seem to be no rules for pets. In a social situation, the pets should be separated from the guests.

When a guest asks if they can bring a pet, be honest with them. My mother seldom allowed pets in the house, then only to visit and in certain areas.

Most of our friends and relatives knew this and it was never a problem. If someone asks if they can bring a pet to visit and you are uncomfortable with this; politely tell them of your feelings.

Many people have carefully cared for houses. A kitten climbing the curtains or a dog wagging a friendly tail and clearing the china figurines from the table must never be allowed.

Business
Etiquette

Business Manners

Here I address business manners—how to behave with the public as well as with coworkers. It is the rumor these days that no one in the retail business or customer service areas displays regard or manners for the public. That may be a very broad indictment; however, I do think there has been a measurable decline in the "please and thank you" department of American business.

It is true that a good attitude can make up for a myriad of ills. As a customer, you may feel you have been overcharged or underserved.

On the other hand, there is an increase in what may be called customer impatience or attitude. As an employee you may feel that all customers are rude, demanding, and unpleasant. We see, with an increase in the amount of income available now for "wants" rather than "needs," an unfortunate acceleration of bad customer manners.

The customer is one side of the simple "please and thank you" exchange. If someone has rendered good service, they deserve your word of support and appreciation.

Also, a potentially heated situation can be disarmed if one of the parties (usually the one that fouled up) calms the situation with a kind observation such as, "I realize you are not responsible for the situation here, but can you see my predicament, and how can we solve this?"

To be calm and courteous is the responsibility of the customer as well as the person serving him or her. Here are a few common courtesies to remember and that will work.

- Never use vulgar or abusive language.

- Never threaten the person.

- Do not act superior or arrogant.

- Do not make derogatory remarks about race, intelligence, or class.

- Do not raise your voice so others can witness you berating this "inferior."

- It is better to quietly walk away from the situation without losing both your temper and your good manners.

- If a serious error was committed and no solution seems imminent, contact someone later who can solve the problem.

Rules for the Public Servant

Here, I am not referring only to policemen, firemen, and librarians. If you work with the public, you are, to a degree, a public servant. You probably get paid for what you do. If you have agreed to accept this employment, then do the job. This may be sounding very old fashioned, but it is simply basic business manners.

• Attitude—Your face usually betrays your attitude, so the best advice is to smile and act as if all is well; and who knows, it might be. Also, with a smile on your face and in your voice, you can say no to someone and they will go away happy (at least happier than your scowl sends them). An important point in public manners: keep smiling.

• Personal phone calls—You may from time to time get a personal phone call that is important and you must take it. This case should be rare. Do not make random personal calls from your workplace, especially if you are a clerk or salesperson and customers can see you or are waiting for you.

I don't know how many times I have waited to be served by someone who was having a great time on a personal call and simply did not seem to have time to wait on me or anyone else. This certainly is poor business manners.

If someone happens to call you at work, simply tell them you cannot talk, and you will call them when you are not working.

• Eating—There should be a place you can go to have a meal. Even snacks should not be tolerated for people working in public. This can make for messy and potentially embarrassing situations, as well as clutter up the work area.

• Chewing gum—Whether this is a noun or a verb it is still wrong. This is the epitome inappropriate behavior in customer service, and it is a real turnoff for the customer. The entire popping, munching, mouth open, saliva-running scene is quite dreadful.

• Fingernails and hair—Grooming while at work is a bad display of behavior. You are telling everyone who can see you that you are not paying attention to what you are supposed to be doing. Plus you are only paying attention to yourself and that kind of public display is unacceptable. If you need to touch up a little, wait until your relief comes or you are on a break.

• Makeup—I have addressed this previously; however, it bears repeating for the business situation. Young women are naturally attractive. The understatement is much preferable to the garish overstatement. If a woman, especially a young woman without much experience with makeup, wishes to add to her color or style, it is well to visit a consultant about color, lipstick, hairstyle, and eye shadow. Makeup should enhance the features or color or natural attractiveness of a person—not simply paint over them. A little goes a long way with makeup. The same goes for young gentlemen with heavy cologne or aftershave and heavily greased or sprayed hair: less is best.

In spite of current trends (which certainly will change), good taste is good taste; and fads and curious-looking new directions in dress and personal grooming are not the correct appearance in a business or trade setting. An attractive salesperson is a distinct advantage to any business; however, to be so garish or unnecessarily colorful as to attract attention to your person rather than your product is not a good idea.

• Clothing—Your clothing should be an under-statement or should coordinate with the job you are attempting to do and not simply draw attention to yourself. The great business example is probably the edict that prevailed for years at the International Business Machines Company (IBM).

At the IBM of the '60s and '70s, representatives of the company working with the public were required to wear a navy blue suit, a maroon or red tie, and a white shirt. This was not an occasional thing; it was every day. The idea was for the representative to look very business-like and professional, but also not to appear in wild and garish colors and sporty or inappropriate attire for the job they were to do. Make it a point to think about what you are wearing or will wear in a work situation.

Some of the bad ideas include tight clothing for either men or women. Avoid revealing clothing, as we mentioned earlier, or very loud colors, unless you know your color well and the accent works.

Equally out of sync with the business community are heavy gold chains on men and shirts unbuttoned to reveal patches of chest hair. It should go without saying to young women of respect and taste that revealing clothing, whether it is very short skirts or low-cut sweaters or blouses, is not appropriate.

The baggy pants and oversized sweatshirts are as out of the picture as tight clothing. Bare midriffs are for the beach and not for the jewelry counter or the hardware store. Be understated, conservative, and draw attention to your store, your product, or the class you are teaching.

Workplace Etiquette

I have discussed manners in dealing with customers and manners for the customer. Here, I will address matters of etiquette and behavior in the workplace or office.

While general rules of good behavior always apply, there are some differences for people who are together all day and almost every day. For a man, some of the gestures he may show to a woman in a social situation would seem over solicitous in the workplace and may be misinterpreted. It is usually not necessary to open doors for women at work, or light cigarettes, or stand when a woman enters the office. With more women in the workplace and with the ideas of equality changing and the situation sometimes very tense, again we should communicate.

If an employer or human resources operative is really in tune and sensitive to his or her office environment, some explanation of the atmosphere or expectation will be part of a new employee orientation.

An employer may also call all the female employees together and ask them how they wish to be treated regarding manners in the office. The employer will probably not get complete agreement, but enough of a feeling to advise male employees on the expectations. In an office or business environment, when it comes to questionable sexual behavior, "hitting on" employees of the opposite gender, or sexist or bawdy jokes, there is only one rule: don't do it. An employee who behaves in this manner can get in a great deal of trouble, and an employer who tolerates this type of behavior can get in even more trouble.

Of course, men and women are different, but in the workplace the treatment must be equal, objective, and professional. Here are some suggestions regarding other issues of etiquette in business.

• Interviews—are usually uncomfortable for both the interviewer and the interviewee. The person conducting the interview should do what is necessary to make the interviewee feel comfortable, perhaps moving out from behind the desk to a less formal setting. The interviewer may also offer a beverage to begin the session and to relax the situation.

The interviewer will want to ask the interviewee to tell a little about him or herself. Not only does this get valuable information about the potential employee, it gives the individual time to relax and prepare for forthcoming conversation.

What the interviewee is wearing is important. The interviewer is going to make some serious and important assumptions as soon as the interviewee walks into the room.

The first thing, and possibly the hardest, is to relax. I have interviewed people who brought with them a command of the situation and a relaxed confidence that made it easy for me to interview them. It also added a great deal to their credibility.

On other occasions, I have made a quick and negative judgment based solely on what I observed. I recall one time when two young women came to my office to present a service that had some genuine merit that I might have wanted to utilize. However, both of them came dressed in black suits, wearing too much makeup and five-inch heels. In addition, they refused my offer to sit and talk, but hovered over my desk like some Shakespearian apparition or a bad dream. I was personally offended by their attitudes and the conversation was very brief. I think perhaps we both lost something.

The guidelines I discussed earlier about dress certainly apply in the interview. You are there to make a positive—but not bizarre—impression, and you wish the person to listen to what you have to say, whether you are selling a product or yourself.

For both men and women, dark or plain suits are in order. Limited jewelry and light makeup and scents are also appropriate. Sit up, exhibit good posture (just like your mother told you), and answer questions openly, with a clear voice.

• Letters of reference—that carry a tone of validity and sincerity are always the best idea. They do not take much time to write or read, and get right to the point. If you write a letter that is too long, it may seem unbelievable, or like you are trying to "guild the lily."

Begin the letter: "To whom it may concern," unless you know the person well or have a specific name. If the letter concerns some specific talents or skills, describe why the person for whom you are writing the letter will fit the situation in question. A person should exercise some caution about letters of reference. Be certain you really do know enough about the person to refer him or her, or the exercise becomes meaningless for both of you. If you are asked for a reference from someone you feel you do not know well enough, please tell him or her politely that there are better persons to write the letter, but let the employee understand you do not take this situation lightly. If you feel you honestly cannot give the person a positive reference, politely tell them it is really the kindest thing you can do.

• Smoking—involves courtesy of the smoker and the nonsmoker. To some degree, it depends upon your own comfort level. If you have a problem with people smoking in your office or work area, politely tell them. However, in some business situations, it is considered the right of a senior person to smoke in the office of a junior. I do not believe this is any longer the case. The issues of health and smoking more often override the comfort of the smoker.

The flip side is, if you wish to smoke in close proximity to someone, regardless of where, it is appropriate to ask if he or she minds.

Smoking in other people's cars or at a table where they are eating is now considered quite inconsiderate, unless they have given permission. The old idea of "finish your meal, ask for coffee, and light up" is not quite that easy or habitual anymore. If this is not an issue with you, it is easy to handle in the office by simply putting an ashtray in your office and letting colleagues know that you do not mind if they smoke. The bottom line here, once more, is more how you handle this rather than what you do. If you wish to ask someone not to smoke or wish to ask someone if you may smoke, being polite and courteous makes all the difference.

Dating Coworkers

Many companies discourage dating between co-workers. Review your employer's dating policy. When approaching a coworker about a date, be cautious. With the climate the way it is, dating in the work force is a hot breeding ground for a reprimand or worse (being fired, law suits, charges pressed for sexual harassment, etc.)

It is often easiest if you have a friend test the waters for you. If he is rebuked even slightly, back off completely; even to the point of avoiding this person for a while to ensure they don't feel you are watching them. Begin your dating approach by inviting him or her to lunch during work hours and go from there. This is a nonthreatening, neutral way to see if they are receptive to you in a more intimate way. By intimate I mean dating off-hours.

Lotteries, Pools, Food & Charities

If your office plays the lottery as a group, or bets on football games, etc., and you are opposed to gambling, you may simply refuse to participate. No need for long excuses or avoiding the topic. State, "No, thank you. I prefer not to play. But thanks for thinking of me."

If your office nickel-and-dimes you for birthday contributions or their children's fundraisers, decline politely yet firmly. Many people don't have much of a social life outside of the work place, which makes it difficult to cultivate outside friends. Hence, when one's child is selling Girl Scout cookies, they decide to bring it to the office.

Firing Tact

Whether the reason for firing is severe or to follow company policy, courtesy still must come into play. This tense situation is not the time to be rude and out of line. Following are some easy rules to follow when firing someone.

- Never fire someone through e-mail or a written letter—this is cowardly and inconsiderate.

- It is better to fire someone before the holidays, rather than waiting until after them. At least let them know that you will be letting them go. Most people would not be so extravagant at Christmas if they were aware that the credit cards that come due in January could not be met as planned. The thinking that it's better to let them have a good holiday will not put food on their table in January once they are unemployed.

- Unless absolutely necessary, do not fire someone over the telephone or by memo. In person is plainly the best way to go.

- If there is a specific reason you are letting them go, it is often kinder to let them know, so that if there is behavior that needs changing, it can be addressed before finding employment elsewhere.

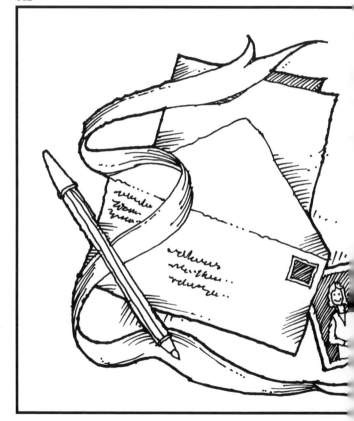

Communication Etiquette

Conversation & Correspondence

Conversation has been compared to dancing, fencing, and chess. A conversation can be uplifting, boring, revealing, exciting, painful, tense, awkward, or comfortable. The first thing to learn in the art of conversation is the difficult task of being a good listener. Any conversation will be less than pleasant if you are not in the conversation as an active participant. If you are not carrying the conversation and the subject is of no interest to you or simply bores you, fake it. Good manners demand that you attempt a participation in the conversation subject if only to learn; and all the while appear interested. If you are carrying or dominating the conversation, stop and listen to yourself. Make the necessary adjustments to keep from boring others.

The next rule is to physically be present. When you are conversing with someone, give them your mental and physical attention. Do not look over his shoulder to see who else may be in the room. Do not look away to find the food or examine the décor of the room.

Years ago I attended a party, at the invitation of a friend from work. The party was a huge affair held in a very nice hotel in New York City at mid day. The party was an anniversary celebration for Johnson Publications.

My friend had just introduced me to Sammy Davis, Jr., and I was completely awed at the opportunity. Neither of us is very tall, and just as we were finishing our introductions, we were aware of two large persons pressing us from either side. Finding some humor in our being literally pushed together, we looked up to see Mohammed Ali and Jimmy Brown holding an unconcerned conversation over the top of our heads.

Walking into any social event where you do not know most everyone is a conversational challenge. There are a few people who have the easy presence to begin a conversation with anyone and move from person to person effortlessly. The rest of us need to think about this situation.

Bad conversational clichés are better left unsaid. Introduce yourself, smile, and try not to say anything completely absurd. Weather is usually a bad topic unless it is on everyone's mind. A compliment on the person's attire or appearance is good, as are comments about the economy, something in the news, or a common professional topic.

Avoid, beginning a conversation on an argumentative tone or taking up a position that you know may be controversial.

The best advice is to be yourself, smile, listen for a bit to see the direction of the talk or pick up something from the introduction and step in ever so lightly.

Personal Questions & Hot Topics

Personal questions are difficult to handle even between two good friends who are alone. In a social situation, keep it simple and light. Sometimes this flows into a meaningless chatter, but that is better than an insult or an offense. You can admire a dress without asking where it came from or how much it cost. You can wish someone a return to health without commenting on an obvious limp or scar.

Do not ask questions about someone's financial situation, the condition of their marriage, or the current relationship with a former beau or spouse.

Unless you are at a political party rally or in a church meeting, it is usually good to avoid politics and religion. Some people come to social gatherings looking for a forum.

If you feel strongly about a subject and are not with people you know feel the same, it is usually better not to get entangled in the subject.

I mentioned opening a conversation with a general comment about someone's general appearance, such as, "You look very well" or "That dress suits you very well." Those comments are acceptable; however, you neither admire or criticize a person's specific appearance, such as, "You have beautiful teeth."

Complaints, Sarcasm & Humor

Here are three more conversational directions or insertions that can cause some real problems, either for the speaker or the listener. No one wants to hear your complaints. When an acquaintance or a person just introduced at a social situation asks how you are, they are simply conforming to polite conversation. In return, you say you are just fine or some such, so they are not forced to share your burdens while at a party.

Sarcasm is also a sword better left sheathed. You will find, perhaps more often than you wish, person's who know no other form of attempted humor than sarcasm. Unless you consider yourself the master of the one line retort do not attempt to answer sarcasm with sarcasm. This type of response too easily misses the mark and is simply offensive. Sarcasm is usually best met with a very mellow and general response or a delicate change of subject.

If you walk into a conversation and feel you must say something very humorous to break the ice; don't. Humor is a delicate thing. When you share a sense of humor with someone, it can be wonderful and you can bounce your quips off one another comfortably all night. If you are not aware of what a person or group of people consider humorous, proceed slowly.

I have an uncle whom I love dearly, yet I avoid him at all costs at family gatherings because I have heard all the jokes he has, many times.

Go slowly into uncharted waters, which is definitely the classification for untested humor. Try all your new jokes on your dog, if he collapses with laughter, you might use one or two at the next party you attend.

Conversation Etiquette

Here is a brief summation of conversational bad manners to avoid at all costs. If you are one of these, take heed.

• The Bore—This one generally talks about himself or herself and has no patience for anyone else.

• The Know It All—Many times at social gatherings you will meet people who really do know a lot. These people are generally quite reserved about their knowledge. Beware the persons who want to play can-you-top-this with every subject presented.

• The Loud Mouth—Conversation is generally a quiet pastime, occasionally interrupted by genuine laughter.

• The Whiner—You may have some very legitimate problems, but a social gathering is not the place to air them. Call your priest, pastor, mother-in-law, or a close friend concerning these issues. However, when you go to a party or dinner, leave these issues at home.

• The Ferret—This one asks the very personal questions, tries to unearth as much dirt as possible and is oblivious to the offense he or she gives in an attempt to dig out more tidbits, while exhibiting an insincere facade of interest or concern.

• The Scanner—This one seems to have a head that is attached similarly to that of a barn owl. While conversing with you, they can scan the entire room for a full 360 degrees in search of persons more attractive or more important than you.

• The Linguist—Regardless of the make-up of the accumulated visitors, this one needs all to be aware they speak another language.

Written Word

I will delve a little into the form of certain correspondence, or the appropriate way to invite, inform, or thank a person in writing. Less is written now than in years past due to the ease made possible through electronic communication. However, putting a thought to paper is one of the most satisfying ways to communicate with someone. It is generally difficult for many to put thought into writing, but it is important to try.

The greatest satisfaction often comes to the one who writes the note or letter or invitation rather than the recipient. You can run into an old school friend, excitedly exclaim how good it is to see them again, and then be gone. If you take the time to put that sentiment into a card or a note, it is possibly retained for some time and the pleasant effect of your meeting is repeated many times as the note is read and reread and possibly kept.

Thank-you Notes

Traditionally, thank-you notes for a wedding gift or for entertaining were prepared and sent by the woman of the house or the female significant other. With customs changing, both men and women now get involved in this necessary courtesy.

The sooner a thank you is sent, the better. By responding quickly, the writer has a more current memory of what he or she is writing about and the recipient is pleased with the promptness and demonstrated pleasure of the sender.

There are times when a thank you is unexpected and a pleasant surprise, and other times when the note is obligatory. The following situations require that you respond in writing:

- When you receive a gift by mail or express delivery.

- After a weekend visit.

- When you have been ill and have received a gift.

- For gifts received at your wedding or reception.

- When you have been sent a letter of condolence.

- When you attended a function at which you were the guest of honor.

- After having dinner at the home of your employer or boss.

There are other times, as I mentioned, when it is a good idea to send along a nice note, but it is not really considered mandatory.

- After a dinner party, especially if it was a fairly small, personal dinner.

- After a business luncheon or other business entertainment.

- After having a successful job interview. If you really want this job, by all means send along a note, most of the other applicants will not.

- After receiving a note of congratulations for a birthday or other occasion. If you receive a printed or commercial card with nothing but a signature, it is not necessary to respond.

- When you have hosted a nice dinner or party and a guest sent a gift. You can thank him by telephone if you wish but I prefer the more polite and lasting note.

- After you have been given a sum of money as a gift, you should send a note very promptly and should mention the amount of the gift and even give some information as to how you plan to use the money.

- When you have been a weekend guest, you should send a note to thank the host for the hospitality shown you.

Stationery

Stationery need not be expensive, but should not be the cheapest paper available. You needn't think it particularly pretentious to have personal stationery for your private correspondence.

There are many choices for men or women as well as for people of differing ages. Brighter colors or any other than a white or cream should be used for less formal occasions. Personal stationery may display a set of initials or a coat of arms if you happen to have one, but should not be too adorned.

Personal notepaper is five inches by seven inches and can be folded or not. There are thank-you cards that are already folded for a more formal occasion.

Having personal stationery accomplishes two things. First, it gives a great sense of consideration and caring to the recipient of your note. Second, it will encourage you to send notes more often.

I recall one time sending a letter to someone from a business. A prominent gentleman had requested more information about a product he had purchased for his wife. I sent a typed letter of information, with some personal references of respect along with extra accessories for the item. I received a reply on personal stationery, expressing great appreciation for the service the gentleman had been given. This note is something I will always treasure, but the grace with which it was sent was even more impressive.

The personal stationery of a woman can be engraved with her name or her initials. If the lady chooses to use her full name, it should be "Mrs. Charles Adam Smith" not "Mrs. Becky Smith." An unmarried woman may use "Miss," though some may choose to use the modern "Ms." or simply their first name.

The personal stationery of a man may be white, tan, or gray. His name may be engraved at the top and can include his address. The address, however, should be a home rather than a business address.

Personal stationery is not the same size as business correspondence. It may be five inches by seven inches or smaller and should be folded only one time not like a business letter. When folded, the letter should fit into an almost square envelope.

Personal stationery is different from notepaper. Both may be personalized; however, the notepaper is more casual and can contain only one rather than the full name.

Notepaper can be printed with all types of designs and cartoons as it is meant for much more casual correspondence. The less formal note pads or sheets can also be smaller in size and any color the sender wishes to choose.

Letter of Introduction

A business letter of introduction is part of the business world and an aid in getting someone a start. Social letters of introduction are not necessary anymore with the ease of the telephone or e-mail.

The thing to remember in a business letter of introduction is that the writer is being reviewed as much as the person being recommended. The letter must follow approved form, not contain a lot of errors, and make the point of sincere interest. I will not go into business form here, the libraries are full of good books on letter form. As far as the point of sincerity, it is a good rule not to get caught in the pattern of being willing to write a letter for anyone who asks. If you cannot honestly recommend someone, tell them your concerns and politely decline. If you begin to recommend too freely, your recommendations will have little value.

Letter of Complaint

When writing to complain, be certain you are on sound footing with your facts and write a concise letter. You want the letter to get results and for a problem to be corrected. You may wish to add emphasis to get some attention to your problem, but be certain you do it well.

When complaining, never use vulgar or offensive language or threats. Be certain your grammar and punctuation are impeccable. A semiliterate complaint seldom gets an answer. Here are some other pointers.

- Get the facts straight and avoid skirting around them.

- Even if you are furious, be polite.

- Do some homework, learn as much as you can about the company before you complain.

- Address the letter to the proper person. Libraries and other business organizations have directories or annual reports with listings of company officers and their responsibilities.

- The letter should be typed with good form and legible type face.

- One more time. Be polite, no matter how angry you are. Chances are the first person to read your letter cannot solve your problem. If he is offended, the letter will probably go no further.

Personal Letters

These are the letters we all love to receive. Whether it goes back to going away to camp or to school or in the armed forces, we all love to get letters, and the more personal information in them, the better. Personal letters should reflect your personality. I have always thought the most personal way to communicate was in a letter (next to poetry, of course).

Personal letters can go to acquaintances, relatives, good friends, husbands, wives, children, and sweethearts. The tone of the letter and the content will differ, depending upon how well we know the person to whom we are writing.

Some of the same rules apply to letters and correspondence as to conversation. The letters we do not wish to receive are the ones from people who bore us, whine and complain to us, boast to us, or are sticky with insincere flattery.

My wife has a friend who moved away several years ago. At the time, the two of them were not very close, but they began a correspondence when the friend moved. This lady is very intelligent and has a gift of putting herself and her immediate surroundings into a letter so you can almost visualize her at the time the letter was written, or whatever she writes about. If she is sitting at her kitchen table in the winter she will write about the birds feeding on the window sill or the long icicles hanging from the eaves. A letter from her is a joy because it is her.

Letter writing is an art and a form of communication that is definitely vanishing. However, if we are to even occasionally write someone a personal letter, we must know how to use the language in which we are writing.

Many of us are still either fearful of expressing an emotion for fear it will be shared with someone, or we don't know how. If you are just going to write about the weather, your reader can be better informed by tuning in to the morning news. If you are going to write about the day at the park ruined by the rain, or the beauty of the falling snow or the warmth of a spring day, now that is a letter. Put some of yourself into the epistle and let people receive the type of letter you would like to receive.

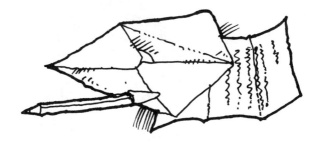

Travel
Etiquette

Travel About

I could almost use the rest of the space allotted for this book to talk about the courtesies and good manners of travel. Many people write of the care one should take in traveling abroad. I suggest that you consider the same courtesies if you are going to the next city or town or anywhere in your own country. We sometimes make the same errors in social judgment in traveling from New York to Miami or from Los Angeles to Omaha, as we do going to Athens or Tokyo. Remember that being abrupt or ill-tempered is offensive no matter the geographic location. You will find that often there are almost as many new customs in some of our smaller cities or communities as there are in rather exotic addresses. Failing to be mindful and polite in Rock Springs, Wyoming, because they do not do things as they would in Hartford, is no less offensive and just as out of place.

If you really want to enjoy a trip or visit, try to learn about local customs in this country as much as you would visiting a foreign land. It will make the trip much more enjoyable and you just might learn a thing or two. Here are a few suggestions.

• Dress—When you travel, dress to be comfortable. It is also a good idea to be as inconspicuous as possible. There is a real economic advantage to this last thought. Many an unwary and overdressed traveler has been fleeced by the locals for attempting to show off how much they knew or how important they were in the big city. Dress for comfort, of course, but don't overdo it.

If you have passed the age when you look good in shorts, give it up—especially the guys in the tennis shorts with the flowered shirt and the black wing tips. Dress for the location or area, but again casual is generally understood worldwide now.

If you go to Scotland, you do not have to buy a kilt, and if you are in Cheyenne, it's usually the real cowboys who will be wearing the cowboy hats.

For your comfort, take note what the weather is expected to be during your stay. Take clothing with you that is easily washed. Cotton clothing or cotton-blend clothing is lightweight and washes out easily.

If you are going to go to a nice restaurant during your trip, take a necktie for the gentleman and a plain but appropriate dress for the lady. There are also blazers or jackets that travel well and are lightweight for the evening meal or night out.

• Talking and conversation—Someone once said, "it is better to remain quiet and be thought a fool than to open your mouth and remove all doubt." When you are traveling your conversation should be as quiet and polite as your clothing. One of the great joys of traveling is what we learn from talking with the people you meet. You can learn a great deal if you are polite and earnest in your questions and not overbearing and rude.

The classic caricature of the American abroad is similar to the big city boy in the country.

Occasionally, you find someone who terribly underestimates the intelligence of the person to whom he is speaking and makes a complete fool of himself and is always less then welcome.

Your conversation should always be respectful and polite, you should seek to learn about the people and places you visit and not boast of who you are or what you possess. Do not complain about the food, the customs, the prices, the local government, or the accommodations. If things are not to your liking then you may leave, but leave quietly.

• Tipping—Errors in tipping or gratuities or showing pleasure with the service we have received falls into two categories: too much and too little. In the United States, a tip or gratuity of fifteen to twenty percent is considered customary and adequate. You may, of course, tip more if the service was exceptional. Don't become a "big tipper" just to show off for your friends or the person serving you. If you are in a foreign country, find out if tipping or leaving a gratuity is even acceptable.

• Shopping and bargaining—Another part of this idea in a foreign country is the old game of bargaining. Bargaining is an art, and few are really good at it. It may be a very vocal practice in some areas or countries and a quiet, almost imperceptible, gesture in another.

Remember, also, that in many countries goods are sold on a very thin margin of profit, and while the seller may prefer to sell versus not sell, give trades people a realistic and fair price for the goods you purchase. The sight of an overbearing and loud American berating a shopkeeper about the price or quality of his goods is an unpleasant episode.

If you truly think the value is not there, simply smile and walk away. Don't insult the person, the product, or the country. The same is true of different parts of this country. Politeness will always win.

It is poor form to spend too much, especially in a foreign country. To boast of how much you can spend if you wish, or to continue to buy what you really do not need, may impress the person as far as his or her daily revenue, but you will not make a friend. I have seen people who were on the boards of giant companies, members of the finest clubs who considered themselves very sophisticated, act foolish when trying to impress some poor shopkeeper of their wealth and importance. All they really did was behave poorly and leave a bad image of all Americans.

• Drinking—All countries and various locales within our country have different customs and laws about the consumption of alcohol. I can recall when it was illegal to serve a drink to a passenger in an airplane flying over a certain midwestern state.

In Texas, liquor laws are by county option, in Washington state it used to be against the law to pick up your drink from the bar and walk to a nearby table.

It is not my intent in this chapter to discuss the peculiarities of liquor laws, but to point out that there are many varying customs both in this country and abroad as to the consumption of alcohol. It is well to learn what is customary and acceptable wherever you are.

In some foreign countries, it is not considered ladylike to drink excessively in public. In other countries, it is the custom to include wine or beer with every meal.

Wine and beer in many places are considered food beverages and are not in the same category with hard liquor. Be aware of the customs. If you are a woman, be careful about public drinking habits. It should go without saying that public intoxication is not acceptable in any country.

The Irish boast about how much guinness they can consume. Australians have been known to describe themselves as a country of drunks, but you can rest assured that drinking with loose abandon in any country is considered bad manners.

A person who is aware of manners and etiquette is also in control of his or her actions and behavior. In addition to knowing the customs and laws of a country (or even a state in the U.S.) with regards to alcohol, know your own tendencies and capacity. It is also well to understand that wherever you are, someone is always watching you.

In addition, try to be aware of religious organizations that may have very strong rules about the consumption of alcohol. Generally speaking, Baptists, Mormons, and Muslims take a dim view of drinking. The point here is that they may politely accept your having a drink, but be aware enough not to offer them a drink, chide, or ridicule them for not drinking with you or appear to drink too much yourself. Remember the first rule: good manners are based on consideration.

On the other hand, if you choose not to drink, you should show some consideration and patience with those who do. Even if you feel very strongly about drinking, some kindness and consideration for others will do more to emphasize your choice than criticism or rejection of the friend who imbibes. Having said that, here is a completely new set of rules when it comes to drinking and driving.

- You will do a friend a favor by being a real nag when it seems necessary to everyone else in the party that someone else do the driving.

- Drinking can be a sensitive issue in many social situations. Both sides in this issue must be understanding and remain friendly.

- You need not do everything your friends do in order to have a good time. And you need not force everyone to do as you choose, either.

Travel by Car

Automobile courtesy, these days, seems to be a contradiction in terms. The cars are bigger and faster, the roads and freeways are more crowded, and it seems everyone is in a hurry to get somewhere an hour ago.

When you are in a foreign country it becomes important to be mindful of rules and customs.

In many places, you will drive on the other side of the road to what you are used to in the U.S. You will have to deal with such new hazards as roundabouts, narrow two-lane roads, leisurely bands of livestock sauntering down your path, and signs and signals with which you are completely unfamiliar.

The first thing to do when you arrive at a new destination (or are enroute) is to take time to familiarize yourself with the laws and customs of the local roads. Whether in the U.S. or abroad, here are a few tips.

- Learn the local laws. In foreign countries there are driving manuals or, if you will be staying some time, driving schools. You may also consult the car rental agency or local police about the rules and customs.

- Know the road signs. It is easy enough to get a booklet about signs and what they mean. Many places use international symbols now that should be recognizable to most anyone. If in doubt, stop and ask someone.

- Obey the road signs. This is not redundant. It is one thing to memorize all the road signs and have the children recite them to you as you go merrily through the countryside, but you must actually obey them. This is a matter of safety as much as it is a matter of courtesy. Also, depending upon the country or part of the U.S. where you may be, the jails are uncomfortable and the laws unforgiving.

- Be calm and polite. If you have not paid attention to the previous three items here, and there is an incident, it is more than likely your fault. Now is the time to be just as sweet and apologetic as you can be. Even if the incident was clearly the fault of the other person and you are the out-of-towner, don't resort to demanding your rights and shaking your fist.

If it is a matter of giving up the right of way, then graciously move over. If someone needs to enter the roadway in front of you, wave them in with a smile. Courtesy, courtesy, courtesy.

Foreign Travel

I will recite again the very basic rules of foreign travel. Courtesy and good manners are the same wherever you are. There may be some variations in customs, but you will find the person who is really comfortable with foreign travel is also comfortable at any event or in any situation at home.

The first rule is courtesy to all whom you may meet or with whom you may trade or interact. There are also some countries or places where there exists a cultural or political sensitivity that you must consider. There will be a few critical watchers wherever you go, so it is most important that you behave with courtesy and dignity.

It is normal to want to relax and have a good time when on a vacation. A good time is quite possible without being boorish, loud, or obnoxious.

A point that simply cannot be over emphasized: When you are abroad, be tolerant and understanding. Understand why things are done in a different manner; do not gripe about it.

The next two reminders are to be friendly and modest. If you are always peering suspiciously at everyone and not making any move to be friendly, they will respond quite the same (and you will probably complain that the people in such-and-such country are very unfriendly).

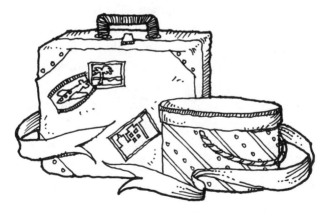

Modesty is always in fashion. In your dress and in your actions, behave quietly and mannerly in a foreign land.

Address people politely and thank them for services. Language is often a problem; however, people really do not mind you trying your high school or college German or French on them if you are courteous and polite and you let them know you respect their language. A few practiced courteous phrases will go a long way in any country. If, however, you are really butchering the language and everyone is aware of it, apologize and try to get by in English.

Generosity also is a relative thing. You can be generous without being lavish or foolish. The locals will know when you have grossly overpaid and you will be surprised how many of them really do not wish to overcharge you.

Social Obligations

I have given a separate heading to a small message for good reason. It is important for Americans to remember the obligations we have to kind hosts in other lands. As a people, we are far too casual with our approach to the niceties of remembering those who have extended kindness and hospitality as we visited them or made their acquaintance. Remember to return invitations and to send letters and thank-you cards to new friends abroad.

Travel by Ship

Ship travel, though not what it used to be, is still an adventure in dining and etiquette. While there are many more cruises than transatlantic crossings today, there is still a need to understand the rules of shipboard manners.

Cruises are far less formal than a crossing, and while we may all have seen the movie, the fancy dress events of the Titanic era are gone. It is still necessary to dress up for dinner every night except the first night, the last night, and Sunday night.

Dress for dinner on a cruise ship may not require a necktie or a long dress. If in doubt, inquire of the purser or social director on board.

In the public rooms aboard ship, you may wear casual clothes, but never a swimsuit. Nowadays, it is usually advisable to contact the cruise line or steamship line after you have made reservations and ask about dress requirements or suggestions.

Deck Chair Courtesy

Again, in a time of more formal ship travel, one's deck chair status was quite important. Now it is more a matter of common courtesy and planning. If you wish to spend time on deck taking in the sun or talking or whatever, make a reservation with the deck steward. If a deck chair is unoccupied, sit in it temporarily until the person who has reserved it arrives. Use common courtesy.

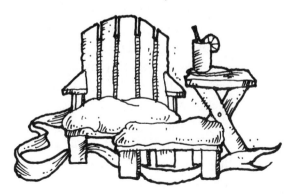

Tipping on Board

There are those on board ship to whom you offer gratuity and those you do not. The ship's officers are professional seaman and are not tipped. Your cabin and dining-room stewards are tipped at the end of the voyage. That amount used to be about two or three dollars per day; however, things do change so again consult the cruise line or your travel agent for the up-to-date rates. Bar and lounge stewards are tipped fifteen to twenty percent.

Tipping porters for loading your baggage can get expensive. People who travel by ship, because of the duration and the social obligations that don't exist on an airplane, often have a lot of luggage. Be certain you put this in your budget. The going rate is five to ten dollars and even more if you have more bags than Liz Taylor. Tipping customs differ on different lines and in various countries—consult the cruise line or ship's purser to be certain.

Friendship & Romance on Board

When you add a tropical moon or the night sky to the smell of sea air, you can truly relax. You should be courteous and polite, look forward to making new friends and acquaintances, but also exercise caution. Sometimes, it is such a relief to unwind, you may be tempted to bare your soul to whomever will listen, but put yourself in the position of the listener. If you realize you have a negative effect on someone else's holiday—quit.

Shipboard friendship, in spite of all the promises to the contrary, often ends as the anchor is dropped in your home port. As you would anywhere, be careful about confidences around strangers. Romantically, be even more careful. The handsome, lone-wolf stranger who just happens to find you more charming than all the on the ship is probably straight out of *Little Red Riding Hood*.

Going Away & Bon Voyage Parties

If one is going by ship or airplane, call the ship company or airline and make certain they can accommodate a large crowd in the boarding area. You may wish to hold a party the night before at a restaurant or someone's home.

If you bring a gift, make certain it is something the traveler can use and can take with them easily. They don't need extra baggage. If you give a gift in an airline terminal boarding area, it is subject to security regulations and possible search procedures. The gift should not be wrapped, and it should be easily identified and stored in carry-on luggage.

If it is a sea voyage, don't stay too long and don't bring a bottle of champagne (or even soda pop) and then drink it all before the ship sails. If you wish to take a gift that will be of some use on the trip, you might want to present it a day or so before so the gift can be packed and be useful.

Travel by Air

Manners and air travel under today's conditions seems almost a contradiction in terms. Keeping one's cool and behaving properly when trying to get somewhere in an airplane these days can be quite a challenge. It often helps to put yourself on the opposite side of the barrier and consider the situation of the ticket agent, the stewardess, the sky cap, or whomever you are dealing with, and look back into the usually frustrated or confused or angry sea of faces looking to this person to solve their problems.

That person attempting to serve you probably did not start your particular problem, so be courteous, be patient, and you will get to your flight and destination much easier.

All of the issues we addressed with the situations of waiters, store clerks, etc., are true of airline employees. Everyone is in a hurry and wants to get going and has probably had one or two dicey little experiences just getting to the airport. It is also true that if you are calm and polite and as helpful as you can be, the situation will be better.

In addition, it is important to obey the rules. Air travelers do not read signs or think that the regulations apply to them, whether it is in the number of bags you can carry on or how many drinks may be served to you. And that is at least half the problem.

If you conduct yourself as a lady or gentleman, you will get much better assistance from the frazzled employees than by insulting or berating them. The only person you have control over is yourself.

When you purchase your ticket and receive instruction as to boarding and the time of arrival at the airport, parking restrictions and the like, please heed them.

One of the thorniest problems facing passengers and the airlines is carry-on luggage. Most airlines attempt to accommodate the needs of passengers, but there are limits. I remember once boarding a flight from El Paso, Texas, and having to ride all the way to Denver next to two sombreros and a piñata.

I have seen people struggling down the aisle with bags that are clearly large enough to be checked and then straining to force them into an overhead compartment that is too small. These people invariably congest the entire aisle and delay the departure.

When you travel, travel with some intelligence. You rarely need everything you pack. The surest way to expedite your way on and off the airplane is to obey the regulations about luggage, get quickly to your seat, buckle up, and wait patiently for others to board.

The movement of the great numbers of people now flying is a logistical nightmare. Now, the airlines do make their share of mistakes; most often they attempt to make amends.

If there is a legitimate concern, there is a right

way and a wrong way to solve the problem. Simply ask to see or speak with the person who can solve your problem or assist you. You may have to be firm; however, remember the difference between a firmness born of being right and due consideration, and that of simply being loud and difficult.

Ask politely for a pillow or a blanket if necessary, thank the steward or stewardess for service, smile when meals or snacks are served, and deplane quietly with a smile and a thank you.

Hotels, Motels & Inns

Staying in a hotel has changed drastically over the years. The hotel stay, like everything else, has become much more casual both in the nature of the accommodations and our approach to the stay. The first thing is to decide where you wish to stay, how long you will stay, and how much you wish to spend. You may be a person who always stays at the most expensive inns or hotels, or you may be bargain hunting.

One of the fastest growing accommodations in this country is the bed & breakfast or simply the B & B. This type of inn has been available in Europe and other countries for years and can be very quaint, comfortable, and charming. In some countries they are closely regulated so you can usually be assured of a clean room and a decent meal.

The grand hotels still exist, and for those, you must be on your best behavior.

Making reservations is both necessary and very simple. If you are accustomed to using a travel agency or a booking agent, find one with whom you are comfortable and tell the agent what your requirements are for a hotel. You must again tell him or her exactly what you wish—don't assume he or she will be able to guess or will fill in the blanks. Also, be very honest about how much you wish to pay. That will make it easier, you will be more pleased with the room, and this agent will be able to serve you for years to come.

The Internet is the newest source of information and sometimes, you can even look at the very room you will occupy and make a reservation. This is now even true with B & B accommodations. My wife and I had a most pleasant trip to Ireland a year ago. Before we left, we had a picture of our B & B in Dublin and a map of the route from the airport—all from the Internet!

The etiquette of making a reservation is the same

as calling a good friend you wish to visit and informing them of your plans. You can simply drop into most hotels and inns and hope for the best; however, it is much better for both parties if a reservation is requested in advance. It eliminates confusion and disappointment.

You may also use a telephone or a fax machine to make reservations in most places. Remember, even when making a reservation on the Internet, over the telephone or in a letter or fax, it is important to be polite and cooperative. I have seen some rude and demanding people who thought themselves very important, end up with some horrid accommodations by being rude to an unknown reservation clerk or bellman. If you wish to be arrogant and self-important, look out; people to whom you are condescending and abrupt have some very creative ways of getting even.

Hotel Services & Tipping

Offering gratuity, although it has become an expectation in many cases, is still a response to good service or attitude. Tipping in a grand hotel will be very different than in a motel, even a good motel.

In a motel where you drive up to the door and unload all your own luggage and get settled is not an issue, because you don't generally tip the desk clerk. Remembering, however, the reason for a tip, if the clerk goes out of his or her way to get you settled or find a better room, he or she deserves some consideration. Clerks don't make a great deal of money. In a full-service hotel, you will usually face a doorman, bellman, concierge or bell captain, waiter or waitress, cocktail waitress, and maids.

The concierge, hall porter, or bell captain can be valuable to you. If you are staying for an extended period, he or she will take messages, bring you mail, get a taxi, suggest a place outside the hotel to eat, and hear your complaints. They are professional, usually very capable, and should be rewarded at the end of your stay.

The bellman, who carries your luggage in and out, should be tipped at least a dollar per bag, and the doorman should be tipped for coming to open the taxi door and seeing you safely into the building (you will love him in a rain storm). The maid or chamberperson should also find something left in the room upon your departure, especially if he or she has left extra towels and discreetly straightened the mess of clothes you left lying around the room.

Depending upon the location and what you enjoy, keep in mind a waiter at poolside who keeps bringing you another refreshment or a telephone. There may also be washroom attendants, someone who will shine your shoes or press your clothes, etc. Just remember who is serving you and reward them accordingly.

Generosity is not the same as indulgence or showing off, so use common sense. This raises the issue of tipping in a private home where you are a guest. When going to a dinner party, never tip the help. When staying overnight and extra work is done in your behalf, it is permissible to tip. In a home, this becomes more of a personal gratuity and should be given directly to the person who has served you. Often in the case of cooks and waiters, they may have left, and then you may ask someone on staff to give them your thanks and your gratuity.

In some homes or personal inns, you may find a notice that you are not to tip the people hired to serve you. An explanation may be given that they are on contract and for you to offer extra would go against that agreement. If such a statement is not present and you are uncertain, ask the host.

Bed & Breakfasts

The B & B is for the more adventurous of travelers. They come in all shapes and sizes, and as I mentioned earlier, are regulated and classified in some countries, but there is a bit of a risk involved.

I stayed in a famous and unique abode in central Mexico where I met travelers from all over the world (mostly young hikers), and we ate at a common table three times a day. The menu was easy: red beans, rice, and scrambled eggs at every meal. But you couldn't beat it for five dollars a day.

A current trend in the U.S. is the "Theme Room" offered by many inns and B & Bs. You may choose a safari room covered in mosquito netting and canvas, a Western room with saddles and hay, a Victorian sitting room, or something like a sandy beach. Other B & Bs now cater to romantic weekends and have lavishly furnished rooms with hot tubs, piped in music, and special menus.

At the typical inn or B & B, the person serving you is often the owner. Your courtesy, diplomacy, and decorum in these intimate surroundings are important. Find the owner or operator and personally thank him or her for the service and the surroundings before you leave. It is also acceptable to leave something in the form of a gratuity on the nightstand or the pillow when you leave.

Often, young neighbors or children in the family will serve meals and clean up, and they should also be remembered in your tipping. The atmosphere in most of these places is so personal that your kind remarks and references to others are more important than the tips.

Differing Customs & Accommodations

There are some hotels that still recognize the European plan or the American plan. The European plan of including a breakfast with the room is still the norm. However, in the U.S., having three meals a day included with the room rate was discontinued long ago in most places.

In the U.S., it is customary to bathe or shower regularly. Visiting Europeans have recently taken a liking to that method of cleansing and relaxing. There are still many places in Europe where bathing is not a daily part of hygiene. This is partly due to custom and partly due to economics. Hot water is still, in many places, a very scarce and expensive commodity. People will in any circumstance find ways to care for their needs. The Europeans wonder why the Americans cannot do with a bidet and a sponge bath, as they do, and feel quite comfortable. Most Europeans are content with a good wash-up daily and a bath at the end of the week or before Sunday. This is slowly changing.

The Asians, on the other hand, make quite a ritual of the bath and most bathe daily. The bath is also a very social occasion in Asian countries, especially Japan.

In Japan, the bath is largely for soaking and for socializing. Before you enter the bath you must wash yourself thoroughly. Many of the Japanese hotels or inns have large steaming baths or pools where you can bathe or soak with many other guests. In Japan, it is not considered embarrassing to bathe in the nude with a number of other people; however, this is a custom that most Americans have not adopted. Even if you wish to have a private bath in Japan, you may be attended by someone of the opposite gender to prepare you to enjoy your soak. Don't worry, just get used to it.

Massage is also a growing custom in Asia, in Europe, and in the United States. The massage is a comforting ritual after exercise, travel, or a long day. This is one of those situations where you leave a tip equal to the level of service received.

I mention the bidet to the inexperienced traveler who will get into a reasonably nice European hotel and ask an awkward question about the extra fixture in the bathroom.

The bidet is quite a civilized idea that I wish would catch on in America. It is a companion fixture originally designed for use in the bathroom after one had relieved himself or herself.

You may sit on the bidet either forward or backward and the gentle stream of water will then cleanse your private parts in a much more hygienic manner than our habit of a great wad of tissue.

The bidet has also been used as a medicinal sitz bath or place to soak one's feet.

374

Wedding
Extravaganza

Weddings

I do begin to speak of the wedding in a chiding manner because we spend obscene amounts of money in this country on dresses to be worn once, food and drink, and lavish and impractical gifts at weddings. But, it is a mother's dream for either son or daughter and woe to the misguided male who attempts to insert a bit of financial common sense into this whole idea of romantic madness.

Now I can return to my romantic side and plan a huge party. The wedding idea may begin long before the actual ceremony because of the drastic changes in courting and the marriage process.

Engagement of Marriage

I must shake my head about what is and is not proper in an engagement anymore. I will strongly suggest some return to the formality and respect of the old-fashioned, "Sir, may I marry your daughter?" type of engagement. In an era that seems to have passed, the intended couple would court in a very public way, avoiding unacceptable intimacy or the appearance of anything out of sorts.

Gifts shared between the couple prior to the actual engagement were kept simple, not too expensive, and never intimate or suggestive of any intimate knowledge of one another.

Now, I can only suggest that this conservative and seemingly naive approach does have a rather lasting effect. The engagement now oftentimes comes just before the couple decides to live together or just after. This may cause some tense moments for family members.

In today's society, promiscuous as it may have become, healthy communication is still necessary if you are to enter into these relationships with some type of family support. If you, as adults, have determined to live together, sit down with your family and have a frank discussion of the plans. In some families, this will be welcomed as a reasonable procedure. In others, it will cause some problems that need to be worked through before the relationship can proceed. Here, I am talking sociology and family relations rather than etiquette. It is, however, quite difficult to arrange a wedding that is going to be a happy and civilized occasion if these issues are not settled beforehand.

It is difficult to manage the grace and poise of the mother-of-the-bride if you are seething about an unresolved issue. Additionally, it is important that as the mother of either the bride or the groom, you manage yourself before your public with grace and dignity.

The bride and groom to be must have a serious discussion if either of them wish the engagement to be longer than six months or so. If one or the other is not ready, there may be a good reason; however, all concerned (especially the parents) need to be told. If for no explained reason, your intended keeps dragging this on and cannot commit to a date, that person may not be a good choice for marriage and you must consider a different plan.

Engagement Announcements

There is the formal announcement of the engagement, and the unofficial (albeit important) announcement. The latter announcement being the sometimes uneasy task of announcing to both sets of parents, or whomever claims the bride and groom, that this wedding is going to take place. In some cases, if the bride or groom has been away or lives some distance away, this may be the first meeting as well as the announcement of intentions. This hopefully, will not come as a complete surprise to either of the parents.

Some communication should have taken place before this meeting, at least enough to know that these two people were thinking rather seriously about one another.

This brings up an event that used to be called the "conference" with the father of the bride. We are still somewhat traditional in the fact the potential groom is expected to be able to discuss his intent and how he plans to support his wife and family. The reality of today is that this is often a discussion held with both parents of the bride and the groom or again, whomever is responsible, or the closest relative to each. There is an entirely new concept of responsibility here.

While many young people wish to be independent of family and able to take care of themselves, this meeting and discussion should be an open dialogue for all concerned about the realities of getting married and setting up a home.

As a matter of good manners, it is still a good idea and a common courtesy for the groom to sit down with the father of the bride to reassure him of plans made and the agreement the two have upon entering into the marriage.

It is also a good idea to have a similar conversation with the mother of the bride. A bouquet of her favorite flowers usually helps the situation.

By this point in the courtship, each of the persons involved should have a pretty good insight into who the parents are and what type of situation surrounds the family. With so many single parents in the world today, and almost half of the young people being raised by someone other than the biological parents, the niceties of this announcement may need some modification.

There are some things, however, that need not change. The groom-to-be should make a scheduled call on his prospective in-laws and express his respect and treat them with courtesy. The bride-to-be should also make an effort to begin a friendship with the parents of the groom. As independent as young people wish to feel these days, it is good sense to get off on the right foot with prospective family members.

Most families and cultures have traditions surrounding engagements and weddings. Many young people choose to get married while still involved with school or training of some kind for a career. In those situations, most are not in a position to buy everything they may need to begin life and furnish an apartment or that little dream cottage. This means you may want to discuss a nice cash gift from family in lieu of a fancy wedding, if it makes more sense.

Announcements & Invitations

The actual plans for the wedding, including the invitation and announcement lists, are handled by the family of the bride and are under her direction. Tradition dictates that the wedding is the great day for the bride, the mother of the bride, and often in a very personal way the father of the bride.

While the groom is an important part of this proceeding and will become a partner in the marriage, the ceremony, the glamour, the festivity, and such are much more about the bride. Sometimes it is the mother of the bride who has dreamed of this wedding for much longer than the bride.

In today's world there are many brides who are dispensing with the traditional and formal and expensive ceremonies and receptions in favor of a simple or even very nontraditional wedding.

Invitation lists can be a nightmare. Very often the bride and groom have supposedly settled on a small intimate group for the wedding and the reception only to see it expand beyond their wildest estimates when reviewed by other family members. I have seen the wedding invitation list completely taken out of the hands of the bride and groom and some hard feelings occur over this initial part of the planning.

At the time the engagement is announced there needs to be a meeting of the minds with all concerned about who is and is not coming to the wedding or the reception.

Many brides dream of the perfect ceremony and reception in a romantic hideaway or quaint little church only to find it is a far cry from the lavish social affair that mom had in mind for the last ten years. The rule again should be compromise, patience, grace, and consideration.

The invitation or announcement should be engraved on white or off-white paper of a good quality that is folded either horizontally or vertically. A white tissue should be inside the invitation.

Many invitations today include a photograph of the bride and groom. Many of these photographs are very casual. However, avoid making the photograph too casual. Present the bride and groom as adults, rather than children. It is my humble and old-fashioned opinion that a coat and tie and a dress are not asking too much for the first presentation of two people together who are going to work, vote, and perhaps raise a family.

The guest list is divided into three sections. The first section is those friends and relatives who will be invited to the wedding ceremony and the reception. The second section are those who will be invited to the reception and the third section is for the announcements to those who will not be invited or are out of town or otherwise will not be able to attend. The list should include all family and close friends, close business associates and even past friends for whom there is still some contact.

The list should not reach so deep as to include casual acquaintances or everyone with whom someone may work.

After the initial lists are prepared by both families, there should be a realistic decision made as to who must necessarily be cut from the guest list. Avoid making the list so heavily in favor of the mothers and fathers that the bride and groom spend the evening shaking hands with strangers.

Additionally, most people who receive an invitation feel a responsibility to send a gift. If your guest list becomes a solicitation for gifts, it is not appropriate. The number of persons on the list will depend on the size of wedding the bride or bride and groom wish. The invitations or number on the guest list for either the bride or groom should be fifty percent. This may vary if one or the other is from out of town or if many of one family live at a considerable distance.

When the initial list is complete it is the responsibility of the bride to review the list, eliminate duplications and review the final compilation.

Here are some other pre- or post-wedding activities for which you must plan and either send an invitation or make a personal call.

One is the rehearsal dinner, which can be a very casual or a very dressy social, I hesitate here to use the word formal. The rehearsal dinner usually includes those who will be in the wedding party, such as parents, the bridesmaids, matron or maid of honor, best man, groomsmen, and such. The parents, other members of the family, and close friends are also invited. This dinner is usually hosted by the parents of the groom and can be anything from a sit-down dinner complete with crystal and toasts to a picnic.

The wedding breakfast or luncheon should also be a fairly select group. By this I do not wish to be discriminatory; however, there are some considerations as to close personal friends and relatives as well as not running the costs out of sight. The wedding breakfast or luncheon in some instances replaces the rehearsal dinner.

The invitations are placed in a white envelope that is inserted into an outer envelope, also white. You may choose to use a pastel color or other clever touches if you wish; however, your best bet here is white on white. Do not type the name of the invitee on the outer envelope or use labels. The

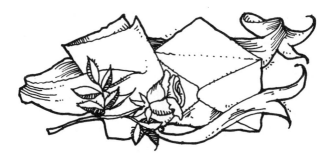

name and address of each person is to be handwritten in black ink. This is true of the announcements as well as the invitations.

If the invitation is to be sent to a single person, it is incorrect to add "and guest." This is too informal and you do not know how many "guests" each person may bring. To be perfectly proper, you need to call those on the list, find out whom they will be bringing and send that person an invitation.

Wedding invitations and announcements are unlike any other social occasions. The wedding invitation can be sent out as much as a month in advance and never less than two weeks. Give guests, especially those who live away, time to plan and to get to the festivities. You may want to stagger the invitations so everyone is invited at approximately the same time (the variable being the postal service) I would suggest out of town invitations be mailed four weeks in advance and those closer, three weeks in advance.

The announcement of the wedding should be mailed directly after the wedding to those who did not receive an invitation or who are out of town and unable to attend.

Many are choosing to write their own invitations. If the bride and groom wish, they may write or have printed an invitation from themselves in a less than formal style, even personalizing it for individual guests. The parents will still be the sponsors of the wedding in this casual style by writing the invitations. It used to be the hard-and-fast rule that a wedding invitation must be engraved rather than printed. However, a printed invitation is acceptable today, with the exception of the highest social circles.

One of the least favorite tasks in the wedding preparation is the addressing and mailing of the invitations and announcements. In a very correct event no abbreviations should be used other than Mr., Mrs., Ms., or military rank such as Lt. The rule is a little more flexible these days. If there are a lot of long addresses to write and a lot of titles, then go ahead and abbreviate, the invitation will still be mailed and received. The names and addresses should still be handwritten on the envelopes in black ink.

Complex Family Announcements

With so many split families and single parents these days, there are also some other protocols to keep in mind in corresponding or communicating with family.

One or the other parent of either the bride or groom may be deceased, which calls for a brief change in the wording.

If the father or mother has passed away and the other parent has not remarried the invitation might read: Mr. (or Mrs.) John Quincy Adams announces the engagement of his (or her) daughter, Elizabeth Anne Adams, to John Wesley Powell. Miss Adams is also the daughter of the late Mrs. (or Mr.) Adams. The same rule would apply if the deceased were the mother or father of the groom to be.

If the father is deceased and the mother has remarried, you may try it this way: Mr. and Mrs. Ichabod Crane of 102 Sleepy Hollow Road,

Boston, Mass., announce the engagement of Mrs. Crane's daughter, Brunhilda, to I. M. Leaving. Miss Crane is also the daughter of the late George Armstrong Custer, etc.

The main rule with deceased parents is that the word late be inserted before the name of the deceased parent.

The use of the word late, and the name of the deceased parent can be omitted all together. Here is another way to make the announcement if the mother of the bride is deceased: Mr. and Mrs. Harry Krishna announce the engagement of Mr. Krishna's daughter, Heckava, to John W. Jones, etc.

Should the mother of the bride be deceased and the father remarry the invitation would simply identify the bride to be as the father's daughter. If it is a situation where such family change took place when the child was very young and never knew the birth mother, no explanation is necessary. The announcement would simply be written as if the bride were the natural daughter of both parents.

In the case of divorced parents there are some suggestions as to how to handle the announcements. It must be made clear, in these cases, that both parents are still living but the words separated or divorced are never used. If the parents are divorced, the mother has remarried, and the daughter lives with the remarried mother, you might simply announce that Mr. and Mrs. Smith announce the engagement of Mrs. Smith's daughter.

If the parents of the groom have been divorced, the announcement is similar; the groom is identified as the son of Mr. and Mrs. Ethan Allen of Salem and Mr. Donald Duck of Hollywood.

In the event that both parents are deceased and the bride has been raised by an aunt and uncle, the announcement is made by the aunt and uncle, and the bride is identified also as the daughter of the aunt's late sister and Mr. so-and-so.

If adopted, it is not necessary to state at any point that the bride or groom is the adopted child unless the child was adopted at an older age and has retained his or her original name.

When a young woman reaches a certain age or is living alone, and both parents are deceased, she may announce the engagement herself.

In the case of a second marriage with older children, it is acceptable for the announcement to be made by the betrothed couple and their children.

Parents Meeting Parents

The most important thing to understand here is simply not to worry about it. Much of the etiquette information in the past assumed that we were all going to marry the son or daughter of the President or that we were going to meet the Vanderbilts or Rockefellers.

It was also accepted form for the mother of the groom to write a letter or note to the mother of the bride. In this letter she was to express her excitement about the engagement and other pleasantries.

While it is still a good idea to send a note of congratulations and introduction, it can also be done with a telephone call and it really does not matter who calls whom first. If possible, it is nice to get the prospective parents together for a personal meeting, but it need not be formal.

Today, with people living so far apart from parents in many cases, this simply may not be possible.

If it is, the bride and groom can simply get the parents together for a luncheon or very small party so they can become acquainted without worry about other guests. Preferably, this gathering is held at the home of one or the other rather than in a restaurant, but that may not always be possible. The rule here should be: be flexible, be cordial, and be sincere.

Announcing the Engagement Publicly

When the family members have been informed, and the personal introductions have been made, the announcement of the engagement and planned wedding is given to the local newspaper by the parents of the bride.

The form of this announcement has also changed, and may vary in different areas. It is stated that the bride's parents announce the engagement of their daughter to George A. Stoddard, son of George Sr. and Elma Stoddard of White Plains, New York.

Some experts used to dictate that the name of the groom's parents never appear on the announcement or the invitation. In most places this is no longer the case.

Engagement Parties

Traditionally, engagement parties were hosted by the parents of the bride or a relative acting for the parents. Keep the idea of the engagement party separate from the bridal shower. This is supposed to be the personal announcement that precedes the newspaper, so it should be hosted by the family.

In the many different family situations with which we presently deal, the host can be someone who is close to the bride or the mother of the bride with the help of friends. This may also be the first time some of the family members meet the groom. At any rate, this is where the fun happens.

This can be a tea, a luncheon, or even an evening social. Oftentimes favors are handed out that include the first names of the couple making the announcement.

It is also traditional in some areas for the announcement to be made by the father of the bride in the form of a toast. If the family desires, a clergy-person or priest may also be present to bless the bride. The bride may wear her engagement ring if the couple chooses to have one, but should not show it off to friends until after the engagement has been announced.

The bride may wish, at this time, to present the groom with an engagement gift. This gift is usually something personal like jewelry or a watch.

Whether guests should or should not bring gifts to the engagement announcement party should be made clear in the invitation so some are not embarrassed to be caught without a gift. Gifts at these events may be general or specific as with a shower gift (linens, utensils, appliances, etc.).

Engagement Ring

Traditionally, the engagement ring has been a single diamond or solitaire. There are many today who choose not to have an engagement ring. One of the reasons is, of course, the expense. Diamonds are very expensive and also very traditional.

Some couples seek to avoid tradition and expense and either go simply with a wedding band or choose an engagement ring featuring a different stone and setting.

There are two schools of thought about who picks out the ring. We all have seen the romantic picture of a nervous young man down on one knee to present a surprised young lady with a sparkling diamond she had never seen. For some that is still the ideal, others think both the bride and groom should select the rings. With the custom sets now available in such unique designs, this should be discussed between the bride and groom.

My advice, unless you know her tastes pretty

well, and know she likes surprises, is to allow her to select the ring.

Tradition, as well as good sense, suggests that an engagement should not be longer than six months, and more practically, three.

Apparel for the Wedding Party

Some weddings have become too casual. I have seen weddings that look like Halloween or prom night and give no one a sense of either fashion or emotional maturity. In my opinion, there is no place where a powder blue tuxedo is appropriate unless that is the garb in which the person wishes to be buried. The black lace trim on a formal shirt should receive the same fate.

The groom should not be dressed prettier than the bride. It is simply good taste to dress, as a groom, in modest black, which is quite striking in its own right, leaving the attention of the congregation focused on the bride.

For a summer wedding, particularly outdoors, a white dinner jacket may suffice.

Bride's Attire

The bride is traditionally to wear white. The alternative is a cream or off-white; however, not too cream and not going into a caste that would look gray. The wedding dress is usually full length with long sleeves, but a three-quarter length sleeve or a short sleeve is acceptable. The neckline should be modest. The time to unnerve and tantalize the groom is not at the alter. Consider the pastor or minister who, in some cases, will ask the bride and groom to kneel. Please be discreet.

Next, I address gloves and trains. It is not necessary, as used to be the case, for the bride to always wear gloves with a long-sleeved dress. If the bride chooses to wear gloves, she will want the glove to be easily removed to exchange rings, if that is to be a part of her ceremony. In a very formal church wedding, a long and beautifully sewn train is quite memorable, but is no longer essential. This is the choice of the bride and, more oftentimes, brides are dispensing with the long train.

Wedding dresses are terribly expensive and many brides today are thinking it is not worth a few hundred or thousand dollars for a dress she may wear once. It is, however, the choice of the bride.

There are some perfectly lovely dresses that can be rented from good dress shops or wedding outfitters. If the bride so desires, she may wish to have a dress made for the occasion.

In many parts of the country, there are talented seamstresses who can make a bride look like a million dollars for a lot less. This is a good time to make a point I read somewhere about shopping for the wedding dress.

The old tradition says that the groom should not see the bride in her dress before the wedding. If the bride and groom have a very understanding relationship and are not hung up on tradition, it may not be a bad idea for the groom to go along on the foray to purchase or rent the wedding dress.

There are a lot of things to consider when selecting the clothing for the wedding party. The bride and groom, in consultation with the bride's family, must discuss the location of the wedding, the weather, whether this is to be outdoors or indoors, how large will the wedding be, what does the bride really like in a wedding dress, and so on.

If the wedding is to be held in a very large church, she may choose a long and majestic train. If the wedding is to be in the living room of her mother's home the train is probably out. If it is going to be 100 degrees on the lawn at the time of the ceremony, she will not dress the same as she would in a cool autumn situation.

Practicality is not always the first consideration when some brides plan a wedding; however, it must be dealt with eventually or it can be very uncomfortable. For all the above reasons it is good for the bride to take the groom into the details of planning of the wedding. Of course, the value of him being completely overwhelmed by her charm and beauty as she approaches him down that aisle may be well worth leaving him home.

Bride's Attendants

The bride may choose a maid of honor and/or bridesmaids to attend her. The bridesmaids' dresses should match. They may simply be the same color or the pattern and style may be the same. The bridesmaids are traditionally expected to pay for their own dress and shoes; however, this is no longer a hard-and-fast rule. Someone may be designated to make the dresses for the bridesmaids. Don't let it be the mother of the bride or the bride herself.

The size and shape of the ladies should be considered when selecting the color and style of dresses. The bride will want to see the bridesmaids before the wedding, so she is certain that all is well in the dress area and the dresses of the bridesmaids are suitable to her dress. If at all possible, the bridesmaids should get together when shopping for dresses or have a pattern and some very specific information about fabric and colors.

Groom & His Attendants

You have the benefit of my considered opinion on the subject of the dress of the groom. Others who have written on this subject take a bit more modern approach such as the inclusion of peasant shirts and vests in lieu of the traditional tuxedo or cutaway coat and striped trousers. For very formal weddings there are still those who prefer the white tie and the swallowtail coat.

Many weddings now feature a variation on the formal theme for the groom. Enough new trends have entered into the marriage dress that it really throws it open to interpretation as to how the groom should present himself. I still feel, however, that this should not be a contest between the bride and groom. If they wish to coordinate their dress that is perfectly acceptable.

The dress of the groom should be enough different from the best man or groomsmen that there is no question as to the identity of the groom.

Colors selected by the bride have always presented some problems for the wedding party. This should not be an issue for the groomsmen or the best man. Pocket handkerchiefs, flowers, bow ties, and cummerbunds are all available to distinguish the groom's attendants and also to coordinate the colors selected by the bride.

At most weddings, especially those that are not really elegant or completely formal, those attending the groom may all elect to wear dark suits and coordinate with accessories. If this is the case, the groom should specify all dark blue suits or all dark gray or black suits. A motley mixture of dark colors does not look at all coordinated.

Parents & Guests

The mother of the bride has a place of honor at the ceremony. She also has traditionally been allowed first choice of the colors she will wear at the wedding and the reception. Some suggest that the mother of the groom should communicate with the mother of the bride prior to selecting her dress. This is now a matter of choice and also courtesy; however, the respective mothers of the bride and groom need not dress alike or even coordinate colors. There is enough stiffness at a formal wedding for all concerned—the mothers ought to feel comfortable in selecting something that suits their personalities.

The mothers, and other members of the party, should consider this a serious occasion and dress in a manner that is not flashy or revealing. The mothers may choose, if it is an evening event, to wear a full-length dress in any color but red or black.

Military Weddings

A groom who is on active duty in the armed services may choose to wear his uniform. For a formal wedding, where the bride wears a long white dress, the groom wears his full-dress uniform with decorations—complete medal rather than just ribbon.

The groom should not wear a saber or sword unless he is a commissioned officer. The exception may be the cadets at a military academy who traditionally present an arch of steel with drawn swords through which the bride and groom walk when leaving the chapel.

At an informal military wedding or even a civil ceremony, the groom may wear a Class A uniform, which includes a tie and jacket. The bride would not wear a full-length gown.

Civil Ceremony

The wedding ceremony need not be held in a church. A civil ceremony is held in the office of the Judge or the Mayor or whomever is performing the ceremony. In this case, everyone should wear clothing appropriate to the occasion.

A civil ceremony does not always mean a small wedding, yet it is a simple ceremony officiated by a civil authority such as a Judge or Justice of the Peace rather than a clergyperson. The ceremony can be held in a clubhouse or hall set up to resemble a church with an aisle in the middle.

The dress arrangements are somewhat the same as a church wedding; however, the party attending the groom does not wear striped trousers and cutaway coats or white tie and tails.

Wedding Flowers

Traditionally, the bride carries a bouquet of her favorite flowers or a formal bouquet of white roses, carnations, gardenias, orchids, or a mixture. If there is no real preference, the bride may consult a florist, giving them the wedding colors, and have something designed that will fit.

The groom may wear a white boutonniere, but never red, and may wish to wear a spray made from the bouquet of the bride.

Many brides today choose to wear flowers in their hair. It seems with flowers that whatever pleases the wedding party or the bride and groom is acceptable. I have seen weddings of people to whom the outdoors or the earth were important where the bride and party carried pineboughs and wildflowers. There are also some seasonal problems with fresh flowers and the wedding.

I have also seen ceremonies at Christmastime

where the bride incorporated the decorations of the season into the wedding party.

Different seasons offer some opportunities for wonderful and colorful floral arrangements. The light greens and pastels of spring, the full robust colors of summer, or the golden and amber colors of fall can all be a part of the celebration that flowers bring to the wedding.

Artificial flowers, even some of the new silk creations, never seem right for a wedding. If it looks like full bouquets for the bridesmaids will break the budget, a small inexpensive spray will do or even a single flower. A wedding means fresh and real flowers even if it is just a few.

Wedding Gifts

It is generally felt that wedding gifts should be given by anyone who accepts the invitation to attend the wedding or reception and partakes of the hospitality and food of the families involved in the wedding. Gifts may be sent in advance, or they may be delivered to the reception or wedding or sent to the home of the bride on the wedding day. It is not necessary for those receiving only announcements of the wedding to present a gift, but many choose to do so.

The idea of wedding gifts often conjures up great ideas of crystal, china, and silver; however, very practical gifts are often much more appreciated. I remember receiving three silver serving trays with various designs or crests that were never used for about twenty years. Most young people getting married are not into the silver and crystal yet. If they are, they may have saved up to pick the patterns they prefer and buy it themselves. The bride will often specify a pattern and guests then buy certain pieces to complete the set. Bridal registries are becoming less formal than they used to be and many young couples are registered at hardware stores, ski shops, or other outlets that either fit their needs or life-styles. Returns and exchanges are a reality of the wedding. Do not be upset if the gift you worried about so much never shows up in the home of the bride and groom. There are so many duplications of gifts that the bride and groom must be left to their own discretion as to what to do with all the gifts.

Gifts for the Bride's Attendants

The bridesmaids or maid of honor will have given the bride a shower at which the attendees presented the bride with a number of gifts. Although this is not the only reason, it is reason enough for the bride to present her attendants with a token gift on this occasion.

The gift is presented when the attendants arrive to dress for the wedding and to assist the bride. Gifts given to the bridesmaids and the maid or matron of honor need not be expensive. They traditionally include bracelets, necklaces, pins, or some other small piece of jewelry.

I suggest tradition is not too important and friendship is very important. This group of young women, however many, will always remember this day and the bride will retain a fondness for the occasion and the personalities involved. The gifts given, although not necessarily expensive, should

be quite personal to each and should have some significance to the occasion.

If the bride so desires, she should feel comfortable in departing from the jewelry mode to give each of her attendants something that is meaningful to them personally. It may be flowers, a scarf, a book, even music—something that has meaning.

The gift for the maid or matron of honor may or may not be the same as the bridesmaids. Usually it is a bit more in terms of cost and has a personal meaning between the two.

Gifts for the Ushers & Best Man

Think about the significance of the ushers and the best man on this special occasion when shopping for gifts. Remember, these are the guys! These are your buddies, they have just gone through this entire nail-biting love thing with you. These are friendships that will last your lifetime. So give some thought to that when you start deciding how to remember them. Traditionally, gifts have included cuff links, silver or gold pens, key rings, or watch bands. These are presented prior to the wedding ceremony. This may be at the rehearsal dinner, the bachelor party, or upon arrival for the ceremony.

Gifts Between Bride & Groom

Traditionally, the groom buys for the bride the most expensive item of personal adornment (jewelry) that he can afford. Many times these gifts are handed down and cherished by their children. However, these gifts do not need to be articles, they can be a trip at a later date, a return to a favorite place, a concert the other dearly wishes to attend, a thousand orchids, or something else that will be truly memorable.

While very personal items of clothing are usually and reasonably excluded, the gift should be something the bride and groom and no one else will either understand or enjoy.

The bride is not excluded from the traditional ritual. She is expected to purchase, for the handsome groom, something gold that is engraved and worn on or near his person. All of this is fine, if this is what both of them want. What I am saying is that tradition and protocol should not be the reason for everything we do on an occasion as personal as a wedding. Knit the guy a pair of socks with his name in red, if that is what both of you will remember and enjoy.

Wedding Ceremony Particulars

Sometimes there are differences involved with the personalities, cultures, and religious beliefs thrown together when a young man and young woman announce that they are madly in love and want to marry. You may be saying to yourself, "What does this have to do with a discussion of wedding etiquette?" Never will it be more essential and never will it pay greater dividends in the long term than that you are on your very best behavior as you plan this wedding. Someone will be boorish, someone will be pushy and overbearing, and someone will be rude. If you maintain your composure, your manners, and an air of quiet dignity, you will eventually have a great influence on all concerned.

A first wedding is a tense occasion. Even if the bride and groom grew up next door to each other, attended the same schools, and went to the same church, there will be unimagined differences.

While the wedding ceremony itself is largely the choice of the bride and the bride's family, remember you are making some very long-lasting decisions. The major consideration should be given the bride and groom in this situation. When it has been decided either from traditional directives or personal preference who does what, get on with it. If someone else has been given, or takes from protocol, the flowers or the food or the arrangements at the church or hall or wherever, leave them alone and let them do it.

The mother of the bride all too often earns the reputation of being a type of "dragon lady." This is neither necessary nor is it ladylike. Learn and use the manners of compromise and cooperation.

You can find a number of books that will go into great detail on the wedding procession, who stands and sits next to whom, and all the like. I will not go into that at this time. There are so many ways to do all this whether it is a big wedding, small wedding, church, or civil. When it comes time to plan your wedding, consult a wedding planner, your clergy-person, a good florist, and others that will be involved in your ceremony. Then you will be certain to get it just as you wish.

Another element to consider here is the degree to which couples are redesigning the wedding. Most religions have a pretty traditional ceremony. Some are very inflexible and will continue to be so. More and more, however, churches are allowing the bride and groom to write their own vows and add other elements to the ceremony.

If one of the parties is Christian and the other is Jewish, for example, they may wish to incorporate parts of both traditional ceremonies into their wedding. Before you decide to do this, however, consult with your church leader or local clergy to find out just what you can do. If, as the bride and groom, you wish to depart from a ceremony that may be not only recognizable to your family but somewhat sacred, you must inform them of this and have an understanding before the actual ceremony. I have seen some rifts occur that were simply a lack of communication, and the parents were not certain that the couple were married when the altered ceremony was completed. Communicate, especially with family members, to assure that this is a wonderful experience for all concerned. It is a good idea to have a rehearsal, so there are no surprises.

What, again, does all this have to do with manners? There is no place where good behavior, poise, and grace are more important than in the joining of two quite apprehensive families. And when all the decisions have been made, whether in a peaceful or stormy atmosphere, and you go to meet your public, put on your best face, your best costume, and your warmest greeting.

Traditional Reception

We have every type of social gathering imagin-
able when we talk about the wedding reception. It
may be a large or small affair and it may be a
luncheon, a dinner, or there may simply be refreshments or a beverage. The reception is usually driven
by personal and cultural preferences.

The big question is often to have or not to have
a receiving line. More young couples are choosing
not to have the line; however, that may also cause
some problems. Should guests just mill around and
introduce themselves; or should someone be a
roving ambassador? Young brides and grooms may
prefer the new type of reception, but it often drives
the mothers crazy wondering who everyone is.

Receiving Line

The proper receiving line includes the parents of the bride and groom, the bridesmaids and maid or matron of honor, but not the best man or ushers.

First in line is the mother of the bride, next to her is the father of the groom, then the groom's mother, and finally, the father of the bride. Why they do it this way is beyond me. I guess that is why a lot of people do not do it this way. It may be the proper way, but perhaps not the most convenient or the most comfortable.

I have seen receptions where an usher was stationed to introduce the guests to the bride's mother. Also, the groom's parents and the bride's parents are often placed with each other as couples.

When the proper line is preferred, the wedding party of the bride and groom and the bridesmaids stand a way off from the parents at the beginning of the line.

There once was also a certain direction given to the acceptable conversation in the wedding line. Of course, you do not make off-colored statements or private jokes no one else understands. Beyond that it should be a few pleasant remarks and then pass on down the line.

Some of the worst receptions are the small-town type where everyone knows everyone else and they talk, seemingly for hours, in the line. Don't forget there are many people behind you who are also eager to give their greetings to the newlyweds. Avoid asking a lot of questions, making sly little comments, or engaging in idle chatter.

At one time it was also considered bad form to congratulate the bride, giving the implication she had successfully caught her a man. One was to have congratulated the groom as the pursuer in having captured such a wonderful girl. It is now perfectly acceptable to congratulate both the bride and groom and wish them happiness.

Seating at the Wedding

At a reception, where there is a meal served, only the wedding party and special guests are assigned a place. Even if it is a buffet type, tables may be reserved with place cards for the wedding party.

At the bride's table are seated the members of the wedding party. The groom is seated at the table with the bride on his right hand. The bridesmaids and the maid or matron of honor are seated to the left of the groom with the best man to the right of the bride.

If this is a served dinner or luncheon, the bride should be served first, as are the rest of her table. If the meal is a buffet, the bride's table should still be served rather than getting in line for food.

There may also be a table for the parents and their guests. If there is no bride's table, then all seating should be open with no reserved spaces.

The parents' table consists of the parents of the

bride and groom, grandparents if they are present, and the officiating dignitary. The mother of the bride is the hostess at this table and first to be seated. The father of the groom is to the right of the bride's mother; the bride's father is opposite the bride's mother with the mother of the groom at his right. The officiating dignitary is seated with their partner to the left of the mother of the bride.

When there is no bride's table, a number of options may be considered, mostly to give consideration to the bride and groom. The newly married couple may arrive just a little late, with all the other guests having celebrated for some time. It is appropriate here to provide a separate, small table for just the bride and groom. The bride and groom should be allowed time to finish their meal before anymore greeting and before the cake is cut. The wedding cake may be displayed on the bride's table, or may occupy a separate, small table.

Wedding Cake

Wedding cakes come in all sizes and shapes. I have seen modest cakes baked by the bride and her mother, others that were small but quite elegant, and some that were carried into the hall by a half dozen men. While seeming to be a quite standard tradition, it is not necessary to have figurines of the bride and groom on the top tier of the cake. If the cake is prepared by a commercial baker, they may decorate it with beautifully colored floral designs of frosting, fresh flowers, or white ornamentation.

The traditional wedding cake was a fruit cake, but that is changing. I know the age-old recipe for wedding cake in England included a very heavy fruitcake covered with a beautiful but quite indestructible marzipan frosting. While beautiful to behold, they were difficult to eat. Of course, the point of the wedding cake has never been nourishment or eating pleasure.

The wedding cake is usually cut just before the other dessert is served and just before the bride and groom take their leave. Sometimes the top tier is removed and kept for the bride and groom, especially if they have chosen to have the bride and groom figures or other symbolic adornments.

When the cake is cut, the bride and groom get the first pieces, the rest is passed to the wedding party. If there is a large reception, the cake is passed to as many as it will accommodate, but should not be planned to necessarily give everyone a piece.

Sometimes the cake will be cut by the baker or caterer and each piece placed in a small white box or white napkin for those who wish to take with them as they leave.

Cost of the Wedding

The wedding expenses are traditionally covered by the families of the bride and groom. The bride's family usually means the mother and father; however, if uncle Ernie is well off and wants to put up some money, it is acceptable.

The bride's family is responsible for:

- the invitations to the wedding and reception.

- a secretary, if necessary, to combine the wedding lists and prepare the invitations and announcements for stuffing and mailing.

- the service of a bridal consultant.

- the bride's trousseau, which is to include her clothing and her household linens.

- choir, soloists, and the organist at the church and any other expenses for the church or hall.

- the orchestra or other music at the reception.

- flowers for the church and reception hall, bouquets for bridesmaids, corsages for mother(s) and grandmother(s) of the bride and groom, and a boutonniere for father of the bride.

- automobiles for the bridal party to the church.

- food at the reception and the wedding breakfast.

- the wedding cake.

- the champagne or other drinks at the reception.

- the bride's gifts to her bridesmaids.

- hotel accommodations for the attendants to the bride, if necessary.

- the gift to the bride, usually her flatware or good china.

- the official photographs of the bride in her wedding dress and photos of the wedding party.

- other necessary items for an outdoor reception.

The bridegroom is responsible for:

- the wedding and/or engagement rings.

- a wedding present to the bride.

- the rehearsal dinner.

- the bride's bouquet, and if he chooses, a corsage for the bride to wear as they leave.

- the marriage license.

- personal gifts for the best man and ushers.

- hotel accommodations for the best man and ushers, if necessary.

- the rental of the tuxedos for the best man and ushers. Sometimes each pays for his own.

- boutonniere for the best man, ushers, and his father.

- the clergy fee or donation.

- all the honeymoon expenses.

There needs to be coordination and cooperation. At the earliest convenience, both families should get together and decide who will or can pay for which expenses. There will be exceptions if the bride has no family or the family cannot afford many of the expenses. It is not unusual for families to split expenses equally or in some cases, if it is warranted, for the groom to pay all the expenses.

Most importantly, as the wedding is planned, it must be done so both families are pleased with the plans and feel comfortable with their responsibility.

Meeting with the Officiate

This meeting is an exercise in marriage etiquette. It is only a matter of respect to plan or schedule a meeting with the person who has been asked to perform the wedding ceremony. It is also wise and courteous to allow a good deal of time for a discussion during the introduction and interview and a respectable lead time in making the appointment. The officiate is at a loss when asked to perform a ceremony and is not acquainted with either the bride or the groom. The minister, priest, or rabbi is by definition, a religious leader to some degree and will wish to discuss backgrounds with the bride and groom. Perhaps the officiate is acquainted with either the bride or groom and needs to meet with the other.

The officiate will probably take the opportunity to give a little marital counseling and will want to know what the desires of the bride and groom may be as to the ceremony; this is to be expected. In most cases the officiate will accede to the couple's wishes as far as their authority will allow.

These days, many young people are choosing to write their own vows and even will ask others in the wedding party or family members to participate in the ceremony.

If the bride and groom have different religious backgrounds, the officiate may also give advice on dealing with this difference and establishing their own rules. Even if the bride and groom do not have any particular religious connections and have given in to family pressures about a church wedding, it is a matter of manners and etiquette to treat the officiate with respect and listen to their counsel.

Choosing Bride Attendants

This subject sometimes seems to take on royal proportions; however, if you feel a bride must be attended, as is a queen or princess, then it is appropriate. The bride may have an entourage of bridesmaids, flower girls, a ring bearer, and even train bearers. The number of bridesmaids is the choice of the bride, but should not appear that she could not make up her mind. Anywhere from four to ten bridesmaids is usually sufficient. She may also choose to have junior bridesmaids.

The selection of those to attend the bride and also the groom should be given some clear thought. There are some courtesies extended, of course, but the maid or matron of honor is usually the sister of the bride. If she has no sister, then a cousin or other family member or her best friend may fill this role. It is also wise to consider the groom's family when making these very coveted requests. Still, it depends upon the wishes of the bride. Those asked to attend her on this most important occasion should, at this time, be those closest to her. Junior bridesmaids are usually from seven to twelve years old and do not stand in the line at the reception or near the bride at the ceremony.

In most cases the number of bridesmaids will depend on the size of the wedding; and it really is not essential that the bride have any bridesmaids. If there is any ceremony other than a civil marriage, however, it is wise for the bride to have at least one bridesmaid to assist with her dress or flowers should there be a problem. Some will make stronger suggestions as to the age of the bridesmaids, but I feel even very young girls, if it be the wishes of the bride, are appropriate to attend in this manner.

The ring bearer may be a younger brother or a cousin or the kid next door if the bride chooses. He is often dressed in white, but in today's wedding ceremonies may wear a suit, a tuxedo, or simply his best clothes. In a formal, church wedding, the ring bearer is to be dressed in white.

The security and the location of the wedding band is of great importance and often some concern to the groom and the groom's father. If there is no ring bearer, the ring is put in the keeping of the best man and he must be prepared to produce it at the appropriate time.

If there is to be a ring bearer, the ring is carried on a firm white pillow. It can either be attached by ribbon or held in place with a pin.

The handling of the wedding ring or rings should be an important part of the rehearsal and all concerned should know the procedure. I recall one young ring bearer who was so determined to do his duty that he refused to surrender the ring to the groom until he received a nod of permission from his mother in the second row.

I love to see flower girls, because they add a breath of childlike reality into a sometimes tense situation. My favorite flower girls are the ones that don't get all the pomp and ceremony down pat. They gaze around at the assembled congregation in all their finery or wave to someone they recognize. One I particularly liked was a little girl who was counting every step and measuring the number of rose petals as she hurled them to the floor as if ordering them to stay where she placed them.

The flower girls can represent either the bride's family or the groom's family and are usually dressed similar to the bridesmaids or all in white or some matching pastel color.

Choosing Groom Attendants

Being asked to be the best man at the wedding is a real honor for any young man. The rule used to be that the brother of the groom had to be the best man. If there were several brothers, then it would be the eldest or the one next to the groom in age. That works if there are two or more boys in the family near the same age, and of course, rules were meant to be broken.

Remember courtesy and manners within a family comes first, so the brother really should be the best man. In the case that the groom has been gone from home for sometime and has lost touch with family members, this needs to be discussed. However, first consideration should always be given to a brother. I say this because of the recent direction taken by young people to turn more to friends and acquaintances than to family. There are other considerations if there are no brothers.

The family is the place to learn manners and they must receive consideration; however, here is where I part with tradition. The groom usually selects someone to whom he is very close at the time of the wedding, or who was a very dear friend at another time. It must be the choice of the groom. Some young men have even chosen their fathers to be the best man. The additional courtesy is that the rest of the wedding party is introduced to the best man and understands the selection. A friend of mine once selected his ten-year-old brother. The youngster never will forget it.

The ushers are a little easier and, as I mentioned, the larger the wedding, the more ushers you may select. One expert has suggested that at a small home wedding, ushers are mostly honorary or to make an even number with the bridesmaids. I have always thought that ushers ought to usher. One of the ushers is usually assigned to escort the mother of the bride down the aisle and seat her. Especially at the reception, ushers can make themselves useful and assist the hostess by directing guests to the refreshments or dinner, seating the ladies, getting umbrellas if needed, and so on. They are much more use to the groom than clustered in a corner discussing the bridesmaids and they can make a good impression on the mother of the bride. So, select ushers who have social skills and personality.

Wedding Photographs

There are two types of wedding photographs—well three, if you count those little disposable cameras that often appear on the tables at the reception. The professional photographs of the bride should be scheduled well in advance to secure the outdoor locations.

This is not the time to pinch pennies and have uncle Ralph take the bride's photos. With a professional photographer, with whom you have a contract, there is some recourse if there are problems.

Another type of photograph is the candid shot someone takes for a scrapbook for the bride and groom. The candid photographs can be included with the order from the professional photographer, or they can be done by a skilled amateur.

A skilled and well-equipped amateur, who is a family member, can often take wonderful shots from a knowledge of the families and an acquaintance with friends and relatives. These photographs are fun and memorable when placed in a scrapbook and given to the bride and groom later.

A popular wedding reception activity is to place disposable cameras on each guest table and as people come to eat or talk, they take pictures of each other. When the evening is over the host or hostess gathers up the cameras, has the film developed, and makes a scrapbook of the most memorable shots.

Guests' Wedding Attire

Weddings and receptions will differ as will the attire. At a large church wedding, you will certainly dress more formally than at an afternoon service on the patio at the country club. The rule if you were on the New York social register was striped trousers and cutaway coats for the gentlemen and long dresses and gloves for the ladies.

The wedding is a dressier affair than the reception for everyone but the wedding party, who will likely dress the same. At the wedding, men should wear dark suits or at least a suit and tie, and the ladies, a dress with a modest cut. The ladies' dresses need not be full length, but neither should they be too short.

It has been suggested rather strongly by some in the past that a sports jacket was no more welcome on a guest at a wedding than it was on the groom. At a formal wedding I would agree; however, there are times and circumstances, especially at small gatherings, when a sports jacket is perfectly appropriate.

The general rule is to wear the best you have or the clothes you would ordinarily wear to church.

The wedding reception is a much less formal affair, but remember, if this is a fancy wedding, call someone and get an idea of what to wear if you are not certain.

I think receptions have become too casual. Even the lawn reception is no place to dress as if you have just come off the ninth hole or the tennis court. The old rule used to be tuxedos or white dinner jackets. That has given way to dark suits or any suit or a sports jacket, for a man. I still think that a man, if he is showing some respect for the wedding, will wear a jacket and a necktie. Remember, good manners means courtesy and respect.

Single Parents at the Wedding

There should a comfortable compromise in the event that either the mother or the father is deceased or divorced. Should the bride's father be a widower, he may occupy the first place in line accompanied by a family member whom he has invited to stand with him. This should be an aunt or grandmother or other female relative of the bride, not a current girlfriend.

If the mother of the groom is deceased, this does not call for a substitute, assuming this has been explained in the invitation or announcement.

If the father of either the bride or groom has passed away, it requires no change since technically neither of them need to be in the line anyway. In practical terms, however, there should at some point be an explanation.

Further Wedding Complications

With over fifty percent of the U.S. marriages ending in divorce, you may well have to deal with split families. Grace and poise will get you through almost every time. If the mother of the bride is divorced and has not remarried, and the father has not remarried, they may wish to stand together in the line—this is not required.

If the mother of the bride has remarried, she may stand in the line, but her new spouse should not. The same holds true with the father of the bride or the parents of the groom.

New spouses are invited to attend as guests, but do not stand in the line. There may be further complications if a stepmother or stepfather has been the actual parent for many years. In this case, it is the choice of either the bride or groom. Let's be reasonable, if the parents were divorced when the bride or groom were very young, and the birth father or mother has not taken an active part in their life, they should not be a part of the wedding line. Get together and work it out—the most important person to consider here is either the bride or groom.

Elopement

For whatever reason, there are times when a couple decides to go off unannounced and be married, then return and make the announcement.

In quaint little towns, it is called "running away" to get married. Many jokes are told and drawn about this, like the father who, rather than go through the financial burden of a large wedding, left a ladder at his daughter's window and money on the nightstand.

We are bothered by elopements that seem to be forced by some acceptance problem between families. Many times when it is known that the bride and groom are not in favor of a large formal wedding, or have schedules that will not allow the time to plan such a ceremony, it is not a surprise to the families when it happens.

Elopements can be planned. The bride and groom should know where they wish to be married.

I do not think elopement is a reasonable alternative to a well-planned and pleasant wedding experience for any family. However, if that is the intent of the bride and groom, make the best of it. If one or the other set of parents is still opposed to the marriage, they simply will not send out an announcement. The new bride and groom may, if they wish, send announcements themselves.

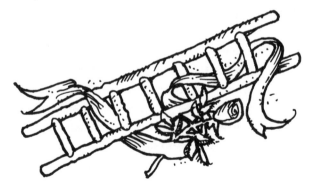

Elopement Reception

Though not in the formal sense of the word, there can be a reception if friends or family wish to have an open house or informal gathering. There should not be a receiving line, however, and the bride should not wear a wedding dress.

Some couples and families elope or condone an elopement for what they feel are reasonable conditions. In this case, the family and friends of the bride and groom may choose to celebrate in their own way and express congratulations to the new bride and groom. Upon receiving an announcement of an elopement, one should not feel compelled to bring or send a gift, but most will.

Second Marriage

There are two things to remember here, one is that one of every two first marriages today ends in divorce, the other is that second marriages have a very good chance of succeeding. There is a significant number of second marriages, and there are also certain protocols to follow for the second marriage.

The differences between the first marriage ceremony or wedding and the second, actually only apply to the bride. A second marriage by definition is anyone who is marrying for a second time regardless of the circumstances of the first marriage.

If a young woman had a young marriage that ended quickly and after many years she elected to marry again, it is still a second marriage. The same is true of annulments. Even if a first marriage was annulled, it was still a marriage. The law may no longer recognize that ceremony, but society is often more critical than the law. Some of the rigid social rules forced upon a second marriage have softened. It used to be the case that on a second marriage, the bride was not to wear the color white. That is not the case anymore, it is suggested that the dress in a second marriage may be white, but not a formal wedding dress with train and veil.

Some of the old taboos of a second marriage have softened. There still may be some differences as to how the bride and groom feel about a second marriage, or even what used to be a double standard for the bride or the groom. It is now acceptable for the couple to decide the location and size of the reception.

Some have suggested in the past that many clergy were hesitant to perform second marriages. That is seldom the case any more. Most clergy feel today that they have just as much an obligation to give the bride and groom their blessings in a second ceremony as the first. There are still exceptions, however, so check with the desired clergy and have an honest conversation before the plans progress too far.

There are some who are aghast at the thought of a second marriage being a big church affair. Traditionally, the second wedding is smaller, less formal, with perhaps fifty or sixty guests and simple handwritten invitations.

Much of the attitude about second marriages stems from cultural ideas in various areas and less with general etiquette. The family and friends of the bride and groom will have input into this celebration. There really is no reason to be less excited about a second marriage than about the first. Generally there has been some unhappiness and a lot of water under the bridge, so friends and family of the couple should join them in this celebration and let them choose how they wish to design it.

The bride in a second marriage customarily does not plan an entire formal occasion with attendants, a receiving line, and all the trimmings; however, it must be understood that if she wishes that type of wedding, it should be her choice, in agreement with the groom.

Another issue with a second marriage is children. Oftentimes one or both parties in the marriage will have children of varying ages. It has been suggested in the past that the children should not attend the wedding ceremony but may attend the reception. That may have been some ancient idea of etiquette, but it is really bad thinking for two people putting two families together. The bride and groom should decide how they wish to include their children.

There may be feelings or circumstances they must deal with, but there should be no general taboo about children at the wedding. They may be the ring bearer, flower girls, or in the case of older children, ushers, or bridesmaids.

Funeral
Etiquette

Funerals

There are two aspects to the propriety of funerals. One is that which is pressed upon those who are closest to the deceased and must plan the service. The other is the need to be appropriate in attending the funeral.

At the outset, I must say that one of the first rules of those attending is not to be too critical of the conduct or presentation of the funeral service. This is perhaps the most difficult time any family will have to endure, and under that type of stress, mistakes are made. Additionally, we find we do not know as much background about friends and relatives and their personal needs and habits until we see some of the requests answered for the deceased. The other variables are religious and cultural differences that we may not know. Be kind and patient.

The need to plan the funeral begins at the worst

possible time for someone to think clearly and remember all the details. The funeral plans should be approved or facilitated by the closest relatives of the deceased. At this time, however, it is often good to call on someone who is more detached from the emotional drain or a professional funeral director.

Many members of the family may wish to have input to the service; however, one person should be in charge. Professional funeral directors or local clergy can help organize the order in which things need to happen and also assist the bereaved.

In many cases, because we are living longer today and more people are dying in hospitals or care centers, many parts of the service can be planned in advance. This may seem a bit cold, but a few suggestions to the family or a discussion with a person who knows they are terminally ill will save a great deal of doubt and uncertainty later. These conversations are quite poignant, but can also be pleasant reminders of favorite songs, hymns, or friends.

Discuss the favorite dress, the flower, the little keepsake. Make and share these plans while you, or whomever we are discussing, is still alive.

My great uncle, who was also a dear friend and mentor, died at the age of one hundred four. He had been a cattle and sheep rancher all his life and, as a young man, had herded cattle in the great grasslands that used to exist north of the Grand Canyon in Arizona. At his funeral his saddle, worn and weathered, was placed next to his casket at his request and honored by the family.

Funeral Director & Clergy

The funeral director can be of great assistance in helping with funeral arrangements. The director is the first person you call when the person has passed away. The deceased is immediately removed from the home, hospital, or care center and taken to the funeral home where the arrangements may begin.

If the funeral is to take place in the funeral home or a local hall, the funeral director will be involved with all the planning.

If there is a religious preference, the clergy of choice should also be called as soon as possible. If there is no religious preference but the family would still prefer a church service, the funeral director can make suggestions. In a religious setting, the clergyperson should visit the family of the deceased as soon as possible. The care of the remaining family members is of great importance in the funeral process.

Proper vs. Personal

Many funerals have a rigid format, though they are becoming more flexible. If you belong to a specific faith and the prescribed funeral is to your liking, you should consult with your clergy and make the necessary arrangements.

Funerals are becoming a mixture of religions, cultures, and personal wishes. At some services the casket is open, at others it is closed. At a Catholic funeral, scriptures may be read by family members and a homily delivered by the priest. At a Jewish funeral, there are certain parts to which the rabbi must attend.

Funerals are quite extraordinary events and are often difficult to organize without certain flexibility. The deceased should have the right to have guests, speakers, and music he or she wishes or no service at all. The latter, however, is seldom because of the many personalities are involved.

With the funeral planning (if it is yours to plan), listen to the advice of clergy and funeral director, listen to the closest of kin, make your decisions, and have it very much directed to the deceased. There is nothing more personal than dying. The funeral should follow the wishes of the deceased.

Divorced Families

The funeral is sensitive and personal to all who knew the deceased. At this particular time, even more than at a wedding, all animosity and arguments should be dropped as everyone joins in the services and the mourning.

Former spouses or relatives who were close to the person should be invited to the funeral and allowed their time of open mourning, as any other member of the family or close friend. If they choose not to attend, that is their right; however, they should have the courtesy of an invitation.

Children & Loss

In the event the deceased person had children, or there are children who were close to the person, they should be included in the services and especially in the conversation and expressions of feeling for the person who has died. The feelings of children should be given special consideration, as the child may feel a special kind of loss and a confusion over what all of this means.

Attention should be paid to the way a child may mourn and the changes in behavior, especially if the dead person was a parent or close relative. Take into account the child's regular activity and the fact that the activity or level of activity may change. It should be communicated to teachers and others at school so they may express condolences, and so they may know what may precipitate changes in activity and behavior.

Children should be encouraged to continue

activities and social life as usual. Older children should be given the choice to alter or discontinue activities as a result of the loss and their emotional reaction.

For the services, children should be dressed in their best or Sunday clothes. The children should be included and invited as we mentioned; however, a child should never be dressed in black for the funeral or any other activities related to the death.

Letter of Condolence

Letters of condolence should not be long or talk about how badly you feel at the loss of the person to whom you are writing. The bereaved will know of your concern and sadness by receiving the note. It is more comforting and helpful to relate a memory about the person who has passed away and some form of comfort such as a few lines from a favored poem. Keep it brief and be sincere.

In responding to the letters of condolence, do not feel that there is a deadline or that you must rush into getting everyone a reply. Your friends and family will understand the situation.

Caring for the Bereaved

Neighbors and friends often rally around a person or family that is grieving over the loss of a loved one. Be careful not to be too attentive and smother the person or treat them as a child (unless, of course, they are children.)

Friends may take meals to the person or the family or they may invite them to their home or out to dinner. Initially any social gathering should be small and involve only persons close enough to the bereaved that there are not a lot of awkward and purely social moments. Later the person or family may feel more comfortable in larger groups and in more festive surroundings. Try to be sufficiently sensitive to know when is the right time to help the friend or relative back into a more normal life-style.

It may be difficult to know what to say during this delicate time. Stay away from cliches; the bereaved hear enough of them from those who are uncomfortable and just want to move on. "Being there" for the bereaved means listening, accepting the anger and tears, and touching. If you cannot think of something to say, silence is best.

In some cases the family may be in shock. They are so stunned at the unexpected event that they cannot think clearly. During this time, it is a good idea to find others to assist you in making necessary arrangements for the family, whether preparing meals, providing babysitting, or maintaining the home.

During this crisis and for weeks after, the family may need to be cared for or assisted in various ways. However, be mindful of their privacy. Don't give out unnecessary information of their recovery to nosy neighbors. Stay mindful of their condition enough to know when to leave them alone. Eventually they will need time to mourn and be with their thoughts in order to heal.

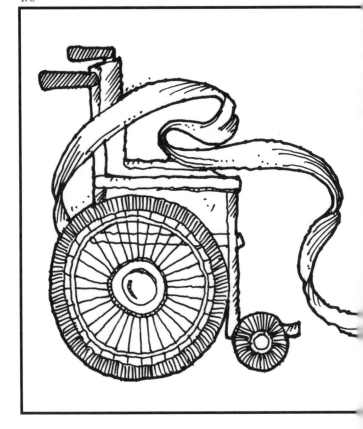

Etiquette for People with Disabilities

Disabled or Handicapped

The most common mistake people make with the disabled or handicapped is treating them as if they were different. They are different to the extent they need our understanding; however, they are people and, more often than not, people that are very capable and often extremely talented.

I recall a meeting several years ago with a remarkable young woman who happened to be disabled. She taught me a lot about the world of people with any kind of disability. The young lady was comedienne and television actress Jerri Jewel. Ms. Jewel suffers from cerebral palsy. She has all the characteristics of the disease that limit most people from an active life. She has not let that deter her and works very hard to educate people about disabilities as well as being a very funny and direct young lady. She was engaged for a benefit performance at a rehabilitation center and had graciously agreed to do the performance. I picked her up at the local airport to take her to her hotel and then to the auditorium. As it was near the noon hour, I asked if she had eaten and suggested lunch. At first she looked at me for quite a long time and then began to recite some of the horrors of eating out when others may not be comfortable with your condition. We went to a local restaurant, had a nice lunch, talked a lot, and I felt very fond of this uniquely talented and very courageous woman. Unfortunately, I witnessed examples of people who did everything wrong in the presence of a person with a disability. There are not many rules you should keep in mind, but they are important.

Any property or devices used by the person should be respected. Do not touch, play with, or adjust without permission (wheelchairs, assistive devices, etc.).

Direct your conversation or comments to the individual, not someone with them. Nothing is more impersonal or impolite than being talked around. These are intelligent people who are perfectly capable of conversing with you. Talk to them in the same tone you would anyone else.

If you really don't know what to do in a certain situation or in general, just ask the person. They would rather you showed an honest willingness to learn than to continually mistreat them.

Do not talk down to the person as if they were a child. If they are a child, treat them as any other child and don't lapse into baby talk.

If the disabled person is not engaged in a conversation with you but is in the same room or area, do not stare at them or, worse, look past them as if they were not there.

If you want to know the details of their disability, ask them. Be polite and please try to ask intelligent questions. Most disabled persons are eager to give others the right information about their condition. It usually makes the relationship much easier. Don't worry about what to call them, everyone has a name and enjoys hearing it used correctly.

Children and disabled persons share an honesty, let them talk to each other. If your children have questions, let them ask. Do not hold them back or seem to be keeping them from contacting the disabled person. If a disabled person appears to need some assistance, ask them. The worst they can say is "no thank you."

Do not pat disabled people or seem patronizing to them. Especially do not pat them on the head; they are not children or toys.

Unless you are truly disabled and have the proper identification, do not park in the handicapped parking areas.

If the disabled person has a problem with speech and you cannot always understand them, that is not new. Please tell them you cannot, and ask them to repeat what they said. Don't just give them a blank stare and then never respond.

Don't feel that you have to search for topics of conversation. Disabled persons have the same interests as you. It may be well as in any conversation to listen long enough to know what the person prefers to discuss.

Not all disabled persons can shake hands. Don't fumble around, simply nod and smile and give them a warm greeting.

While you can be honest about the disability, do not focus on the problem. Direct your attention to the individual. You may find a delightful friend. Just as in any other social situation, when mistakes are made, simply offer an apology, correct the problem, and move on. Avoid negative words like cripple, victim, sick, diseased, etc. Use terms such as disabled, handicapped, or wheelchair-bound. When speaking to a disabled person, get on eye level, it will put both of you more at ease.

If something like furniture is obviously blocking the path or progress of a disabled person or someone in a wheelchair, simply move the obstacle.

Relax and just be yourself. Very often one of the major problems facing the disabled is the rest of us. Remember all the normal rules of etiquette and good manners still apply. Compliment them honestly, do not give false praise—no one will see through that quicker than a disabled person.

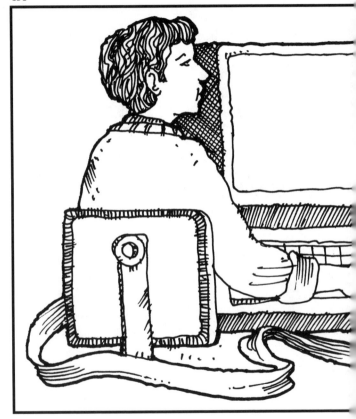

Netiquette

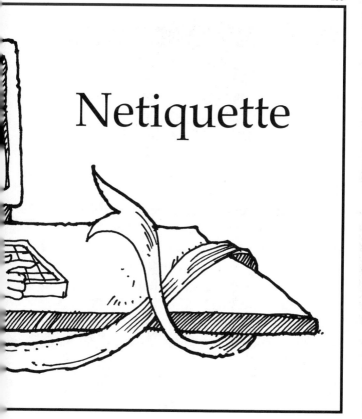

E-mail Common Sense

New technology always presents us with some new challenges in personal relationships. Sometimes new technology has the misfortune of reducing the propriety or the kindness of the communication. Telegrams became a very poor form of communication due to the abbreviated nature of the text. This of course was an economic factor as unnecessary words cost extra money. It also created some very bad habits. Our telephone manners have also suffered over the years in attempting to speed up the conversation or the communication. E-mail is now the newest and the hottest form of instant communication. It really is not mail in the correct sense of the word, as nothing is mailed or delivered between parties. The new electronic communications offer some real pitfalls, such as misunderstanding, interception, incomplete information, and subtle nuances that are not applicable in the electronic medium. E-mail has become a literal flood in some instances, causing a great deal of difficulty for the postal department, because of the amount of business they are losing. There are other difficulties for those who send and receive the messages. Most people assume the message will be read as it is received. Many people actually get hundreds of messages each day and must choose which they answer immediately and which can wait or be discarded. There are, again a few suggested rules that will make the communication easier and more acceptable.

If you want your e-mail read, use a specific subject line. There is no need to be cute or creative. Just send the message and be concise. If you change the topic in the sentence, change it also in the subject line, and be consistent with this. Know to whom you are sending your message and don't send chatty and pointless mail unless this is a good friend who has time to read it.

As with any business communication, when you do have a legitimate message be brief. The person receiving this message may not have time to read a long message or may not be interested in the subject. This goes back to the point of knowing who is going to receive the message. It is a rule of business communication to be certain the person receiving your message is the person to whom you need to speak.

Do not forward or send alert stories, sermons, or other messages, unless you are certain the receiver wants to receive them. Never forward a lot of newsletter items, chances are if the person is not a subscriber, they are not interested.

SHOUTING in uppercase letters or using excessive exclamation points are never acceptable and will usually get your e-mail trashed if you use them in the subject line. Don't use them in the text either because they are considered rude.

Be as polite as you would be in a normal written

letter or in a conversation. Don't give a short, abrupt, or rude answer if it is not what you would usually do. Remember what we said about telegrams. E-mail is not a telegram, use correct form and grammar.

Do not send HTML e-mail unless someone requests it. HTML can be read by all e-mail programs or servers, and it takes longer to download. Fancy colored fonts and the like can even crash an e-mail program. This cuteness gone awry does not leave a good and lasting impression.

Always use the automated quote but also edit it. Don't quote every word of every e-mail when you reply. Keep the message to a minimum so the receiver can see at a glance what has gone on before in the conversation.

When you return an e-mail, don't reply to everyone the e-mail was sent to unless you absolutely have to. If you forward an e-mail and it has been forwarded to you, remove the ">" before each line.

This reformatting is simple to do in most e-mail programs; simply check your spelling and grammar; proofread. If you are writing about a subject that could be misunderstood, let it cool for a period before reading it again. Avoid intentionally inflaming anyone.

Remember that e-mail is not necessarily private. If you would not say something to a person's face, it is best not to say it in an e-mail. Your boss, the server's administrator, the person you are e-mailing, all have access to your e-mail.

If you use a signature, keep it short and relevant. ASCII pictures and ultralong signatures can make your e-mail feel intrusive. Be aware of this if you are posting to lists or forums.

Since the internet by definition is international, intercultural, and inter- almost everything, be careful not to offend others. Religious, racial, political, and cultural remarks, even made in innocence, can hurt feelings and anger someone, somewhere.

Sign your name. Just because it is your account does not mean that it is you writing the e-mail. Also, it is simply good manners.

Do not "spam". That awful four-letter word makes more enemies than friends. Even when it is targeted, the returns are low. The majority of people resent unsolicited advertising, especially if they have to wait for it to download.

Use emotocons, those helpful ASCII characters that symbolize a smile or a frown or other expressions. Here are a few.

- :) or :-) Smile

- ;) or ;-) Wink

- : P Sticking out your tongue (only to close friends)

- : (or :- (Frown or sad face

- @ > -> - Kudos or congratulations (a flower)

E-mail will probably never replace the phone or regular mail; however, it fills a need in our world for quick, direct, enjoyable, and even intense communication with people around the world. E-mail may change the priority of communications and replace or greatly reduce the volume of more traditional forms of correspondence.

Summary: The Author's Top Ten List

It seems that lists are very much in favor these days, and a way of abbreviating our meaning or intent. I will add mine to the long list of lists. In preparing a list, I am indeed lending a priority to the various actions, dress, or behavior of human beings in their relationships with each other. You certainly do not have to agree with me on these, but here is a shot at what I think is important in the world of manners.

1. Table Manners. There are few actions that will mark you as someone who really does not have much consideration for others in your presence as will bad table manners. Unfortunately people will draw some final conclusions about your abilities and your character by the way you present yourself at a meal—formal or informal.

Don't talk with food in your mouth, don't slurp soup, keep your elbows off the table, know how to use the utensils that surround your plate, eat slowly, and say please and thank you when asking for food to be passed to you.

2. Speech. Speech and language define who you are. Speech is the window or perhaps the door to the intellect. Young people should take special note of this attribute or the lack of same. When you are beginning the social experiment of life and the game of work and relationships, this becomes most important. Too many people depend on others to decipher or overlook their local speech patterns, slang, and just plain ignorance of the rules. You may think it clever or even necessary to subscribe to the speech patterns of a neighborhood or a region or a social group; however, when it comes time to broaden your outlook or even your world, bad or vulgar speech patterns or habits will be obvious.

3. How You Treat a Lady. This is for the young men, but it does have a flip side for the ladies. If you want to be treated like a lady, you must behave like a lady. Ask how a lady wishes to be treated. Help her in and out of a car. Open a door. Speak politely. Help her on and off with her coat. If these traditional acts are not to the liking or comfort of a more modern woman, still treat her with respect and consideration. Some women will perhaps suggest that they not be treated in a protective or old-fashioned way, or may feel that the man is being patronizing. However, if the man is sincere and a real gentleman, the lady will certainly remember him.

4. Being a Lady. Most men want a female acquaintance, friend, or relative to act feminine. I do know women who think they have to talk like men, swear like men, and drink like men.

While there is no excuse for a man to be abusive

or sexually inappropriate with a woman, women must be certain they have not left signals that can be misconstrued. If a woman does not wish to be thought of as a lady, that is her business. If she does, she must be especially careful of her speech, dress, and drinking habits.

5. Modest Dress. A true lady and gentleman do not wish to call undue attention to themselves and will dress modestly. This includes clothing that is not too flashy, too tight, too short, too revealing, or too bizarre. Modesty includes not accentuating the negative or trying to be twenty years younger than you actually are. Modesty includes clothing that is well suited to you, whether it is the fashion or not.

6. Alcohol. There are some social circles where the use and consumption of alcoholic drinks is taught at an early age. The use of alcohol as a social beverage is important. It is acceptable to politely refuse a drink or even to explain why you do not wish to drink. It is never acceptable to become intoxicated in public, which includes a small party. As with all good manners, avoid excess and keep yourself in control of your situation.

7. Ugly American. We constantly travel to cultures much older than ours, from which we can learn much; however, there are always a certain number of persons who don't get the message. When you are abroad, take the time to learn the customs and the rules. Respect the local customs, whether you may agree with them or not, be polite, talk softly, ask questions and learn, and leave the flag-waving at home. Do not attempt to throw either your money or your influence about. Be conservative and reasonable in your dress.

Americans are second only to the Japanese in their attempt to take photographs of absolutely everything. Be aware of sensitivities in any country. Some people do not wish to have their picture taken for religious or superstitious reasons. There are shrines in many countries that are off limits. You should also avoid military installations, border guards, and most public officials in other countries.

8. Correspondence & Writing. The greatest offenders are those who do not bother to send a note of thank you after a gift or event. There is an added personal touch in a handwritten letter or thank-you note. Handwritten does include typed or word processed messages, but they are to be hand-signed and mailed. There is a thought process and a reflection involved in sitting down and taking the time to write someone a personal letter that you get nowhere else. Also the thrill of getting a letter in the mail and then sharing the words of a dear friend or relative still makes the day of most people. It is nice to spend enough time with the language in which you are writing to be able to improve your written communication skills. The very personal and well-written letter is still scrapbook material to most people who are fortunate enough to receive them.

9. Family Manners in the Home. Charity does begin at home and so do good manners. If manners are not taught and expected in the home, it becomes very difficult for the person to learn or assume any degree of civil behavior later in life. Parents should teach the basics of dress, table manners, discreet language, how to greet strangers, and how to receive guests in the home. There ought to be some real expectations about behavior outside the home and in social situations.

Guests and strangers are not the only ones to whom the young person should relate with good manners. Other members of the family, regardless of the usual rivalries that develop, should be treated as well as are guests. Good behavior bears great dividends in the home and in all the areas of a person's life that will come after they leave home.

10. General Tipping. A reasonable gratuity is fifteen to twenty percent. Take the time to know the rules, especially in foreign countries, and honestly and graciously reward those who extend good service. Some people believe that you tip regardless of the quality of service. In many cases, this is true for food preparation persons or valet people who pick up and return clothing without ever talking to you. The reverse of that is that a tip should be definitely withheld for poor service or a poor attitude on the part of the person who is supposed to be delivering a service.

Tipping can also be overdone. Avoid the "big spender" attitude at all costs, they may take your money, but you get little respect in return.

Index

Bibliography

1 Michalak, Stanley J., Jr., Microsoft Encarta Encyclopedia
2 Soergel, Phillip M., Microsoft Encarta Encyclopedia 2000
Carpenter, Lucien O., Universal Dancing Master 1880
Compton's Encyclopedia online, 1998, The Learning Company
Ford, Charlotte Book of Modern Manners, Simon and Schuster 1980
Grosse, Richard, Dating Etiquette, www.cupidnet.com 1995
Inlove.org/etiquette.htm Steinmets/Mcfarlane 1999–2000
Members.aol.com/Eastlynne/etiquette.htm
Post, Elizabeth L., Emily Post's Etiquette, Funk and Wagnalls, 1965
Post, Peggy, Good Housekeeping Etiquette for Today
Thornwell, Emily The Lady's Guide to Perfect Gentility, 1853
Vanderbilt, Amy Complete Book of Etiquette, Doubleday, 1978
www.askjeeves.com
www.ecetuveplanet.com
www.tipping.org/tipping/tipping.html

If you liked this book, you'll love this series:

Little Giant Encyclopedia of Aromatherapy • Little Giant Encyclopedia of Baseball Quizzes • Little Giant Encyclopedia of Card & Magic Tricks • Little Giant Encyclopedia of Card Games • Little Giant Encyclopedia of Card Games Gift Set • Little Giant Encyclopedia of Checker Puzzles • Little Giant Encyclopedia of Dream Symbols •Little Giant Encyclopedia of Etiquette • Little Giant Encyclopedia of Fortune Telling • Little Giant Encyclopedia of Gambling Games • Little Giant Encyclopedia of Games for One or Two • Little Giant Encyclopedia of Handwriting Analysis • Little Giant Encyclopedia of Home Remedies • Little Giant Encyclopedia of IQ Tests • Little Giant Encyclopedia of Logic Puzzles • Little Giant Encyclopedia of Lucky Numbers • Little Giant Encyclopedia of Magic • Little Giant Encyclopedia of Mazes • Little Giant Encyclopedia of Meditations & Blessings • Little Giant Encyclopedia of Mensa Mind-Teasers • Little Giant Encyclopedia of Names • Little Giant Encyclopedia of Natural Healing • Little Giant Encyclopedia of One-Liners • Little Giant Encyclopedia of Palmistry • Little Giant Encyclopedia of Proverbs • Little Giant Encyclopedia of Puzzles • Little Giant Encyclopedia of Runes • Little Giant Encyclopedia of Spells & Magic • Little Giant Encyclopedia of Superstitions • Little Giant Encyclopedia of Toasts & Quotes • Little Giant Encyclopedia of Travel & Holiday Games • Little Giant Encyclopedia of UFOs • Little Giant Encyclopedia of Wedding Toasts • Little Giant Encyclopedia of Word Puzzles • Little Giant Encyclopedia of the Zodiac

Available at fine stores everywhere.